relationship
economics

Transform Your Most
Valuable Business
Contacts into Personal
and Professional Success

David Nour

John Wiley & Sons, Inc.

Published by John Wiley & Sons, Inc., Hoboken, New Jersey.
Published simultaneously in Canada.

Relationship Economics, Relationship Currency, Reputation Capital, and Professional Net Worth are trademarks of BeOne Now, Inc.

For general information on our other products and services or for technical support, please contact our Customer Care Department within the United States at (800) 762-2974, outside the United States at (317) 572-3993 or fax (317) 572-4002.

Designations used by companies to distinguish their products are often claimed by trademarks. In all instances where the author or publisher is aware of a claim, the product names appear in Initial Capital letters. Readers, however, should contact the appropriate companies for more complete information regarding trademarks and registration.

Wiley also publishes its books in a variety of electronic formats. Some content that appears in print may not be available in electronic books. For more information about Wiley products, visit our web site at www.wiley.com.

Library of Congress Cataloging-in-Publication Data:
Nour, David, 1968-
   Relationship economics: transform your most valuable business contacts into personal and professional success/David Nour.
      p. cm.
   Includes bibliographical references and index.
   ISBN 978-0-470-28960-0 (cloth)
1. Social networks—Economic aspects. 2. Social capital (Sociology)—Economic aspects.
3. Business networks. I. Title.
   HM741.N68 2008
   650.1'3—dc22

                                                                    2008012193

Printed in the United States of America

10 9 8 7 6 5 4 3 2 1

Contents

Acknowledgments

As we embark on a new chapter in the evolution of BeOne Now, Inc., I am indebted to the many clients of the past and present, who have allowed me to identify and hone a passion for relationships and the craft of helping their teams realize the enormous power and potential of the same. Their trust continues to fuel my aspirations yet.

Likewise, I owe a great deal to our past and present dedicated team of professionals who I am proud to call colleagues and friends. In particular, my business partner, Jennifer Whitt, PMP, who continues to provide love, support, and "centered" fine tuning. If we are all products of the advice we take, I would remiss not to mention my past leaders such as Bill Neal, Lee Nicholson, Ken Marcks, Bruce Kasanoff, and Christian Gheorghe; over the past three decades they, along with countless others, have provided invaluable investments and insights into my personal and professional development.

My thanks go to Alan Weiss, a mentor and one of the best minds in the relationship business; Charlie Paparelli, Dan Brown, Dale Jones, and Paul Young for the purity of their faith in refilling my cup; Veronica Tompkins for her branding brilliance and infectious kindness; Scotty Fletcher for her late nights of editing; my agent Bill Gladstone for his representation; and to Matt Holt, executive editor at John Wiley & Sons, Inc., and his team, for supporting this endeavor.

My deepest gratitude to my parent, Manouchehr and Nayareh, in Iran, who so unselfishly gave up their son to live the American dream; to Uncle Ken, Aunt Jan, Uncle Taghi, Aunt Badry, and Brother Brian for opening their lives and encouraging the passion to dream with the discipline to execute; to my sister Hanieh—I miss you every day and see your zest for life and kind soul in Grayson's eyes; I know you're looking down on our family with love and pride.

Finally, I dedicate this book to Wendy, Grayson, and Justus. Without your unconditional love and support, I would have never finished this project.

Foreword
The Strategic Value
of Business Relationships

I've long observed that consulting is a relationship business. But then, so are most businesses. Relationships vary in their degree, scope, tenure, and value. Too often, we tend to spend time with people who can't say "yes," but can say "no." So what do they eventually say? "No!"

Yet the true nature of strategic business relationships is win/win. This is not a zero-sum game, nor a competition, nor a hydraulic system. It is about reciprocity in relationship building, while also making sure that you achieve your own best interests.

Organizations move forward by building on strength, not by correcting weakness. Strategic relationship management is an underappreciated, underutilized strength that most firms can begin building on immediately with no capital investment whatsoever.

Relationships have value. If you don't believe that, think about the worth of a referral from a business colleague who sent business your way with no cost of acquisition whatsoever. What if that business renews with you for five years, and that relationship provides four more new, analogous business relationships through referrals?

If you think that's far-fetched, talk to any veteran, successful business owner and you'll soon be disabused of the myth. *I can trace over 90 percent of all my current business in a seven-figure consulting practice to four early relationships.* Most of us who are enjoying great success can cite similar dynamics. I've been in business for 25 years. I haven't made a cold call in 10 years or more.

There is a huge and appropriate emphasis on branding today. But branding is simply a form of creating high-value relationships through the consistent representation of uniform quality. I've long advised consultants and other professional service providers that logic makes people think, but emotion makes them act. Brands form emotional connections. Relationships are the most essential conductors of emotion.

We buy, hire, employ, heed, support, and are loyal to those we trust, those who take interest in us, and those who appeal to our own self-interest (which they apparently share). So the question becomes this: Are we identifying, nurturing, and retaining *those relationships which are most important for our business?* Not all customers are created equal. We must differentiate among those relationships which are the most vital for the growth of our enterprise.

David Nour, with whom I've worked collegially for years, raises this pursuit to an art form. He recognizes the value of differing potential relationships, but also delves into how to identify, nurture, and capitalize on them.

Where else do you find that kind of potential source of life within your own organization? This book is your divining rod.

—ALAN WEISS, Ph.D.,
Author, *Million Dollar Consulting*

Preface

My journey began almost 40 years ago, when my dad would walk me through the bazaars of Iran during our Friday errands. I didn't understand the notion of relationship economics then, but certainly do now. Dad got things done whether we needed a plumber at the house that afternoon or access to an influential politician by leveraging his most valuable relationships in the very real and thriving global *favor economy*.

In this turbulent time of global tension among cultural nuances, multicultural management teams must execute seamlessly in an environment of increasingly more sophisticated and demanding global clients. This book is a how-to guide. Its applications go beyond just getting and giving business cards, working a room, or getting the most out of a conference. Its focus is how to strategically invest in relationships as your single and most valuable asset.

I have interviewed over 1,000 managers, directors, and executives of *Fortune* 500 organizations, midmarket companies, and early-stage ventures. They all concur, without exception, that beyond educational foundation and professional pedigree, your personal and professional success depends on the diversity and quality of your relationships. Yet most of us don't spend enough time building and nurturing the key relationships that we need to achieve success. That's where relationship economics will create a far greater return on your relationship investments.

The academic notion of relationship economics, inspired by the famous British economist Ronald Coase and Nobel Prize–winning economist and political philosopher Friedrich Hayek, uses economic tools to study variables traditionally focused on by sociologists. The practical notion of relationship economics isn't about networking. It's about learning how to invest in people for an extraordinary return. It's about exchanging *relationship currency*, accumulating *reputation capital*, and building *professional net worth*. It's about learning the art and *science* of transforming your most valuable relationships into execution, performance, and results.

During my business trips to Beijing, Dubai, and Cape Town, I am often reminded that the rest of the world builds relationships first, *before* they do business. As businesspeople from the United States, we're so focused on the business that *if, and only if,* that goes well, we'll think about the relationship part! Even the very language used in other countries highlights the importance that is placed on building these connections.

In Arabic, for example, the literal translation of *bin* means *son of.* One's genealogy, sources of referrals, and collective cultural history carries more weight toward business success in many parts of the world than any product or service you represent, access you desire, or project you're trying to complete. In China, *guanxi* (pronounced *guan-shi*) literally means *relationships* and is understood to be the network of relationships among various parties that cooperate and support one another. Beyond the perceived advantages of an organization's products or services, with the right *guanxi,* an organization in China minimizes risks, frustrations, and disappointments when doing business, determines its competitive standing in the long run with the relevant Chinese authorities, and minimizes the inevitable risks, barriers, and setups one will encounter.

In essence, relationships are the gateway to business in the rest of the world in contrast to the United States, where business is often the gateway to relationships. The world economy does not understand our the-cart-before-the-horse tactics. In too many global circles, our tactics appear insincere, shortsighted, and even flat-out rude.

By understanding and developing the three types of relationships—*personal, functional,* and *strategic,* you hone critical skills to not only develop a nose for identifying great opportunities, but also for determining which relationships to tap for execution, performance, and results. Personal relationships are the easiest for most; they're the ones you build at home, at your kids' soccer games, at school, and with your favorite charity friends. These are people who like you for who you are, and your interactions with them take place in a fairly safe environment for exposing personal challenges and seeking insights. The obstacle for many is the inability to link personal relationships to overcoming corporate leadership challenges.

Functional relationships are likewise easily understood—they are those you build at work to perform your daily functions. They're formed with peers, subordinates, and superiors and include your exchanges with customers and suppliers distinctly focused on getting tasks at hand completed. The relationship members are usually mandated by your function, job description, and key corporate initiatives, all of which are typically driven by others. You build functional relationships with those who can support your efforts or help you overcome obstacles. Although they are practical for the time being, this relationship building has little foresight and tends to keep us busy with the urgent tasks on our respective to-do lists.

The transactional collaborations simply won't enable you to "see over the corporate horizon" or around corporate corners. They will not allow you to see faint emerging trends before your competition or alert you to early warning signals that may threaten your markets.

Unfortunately, strategic relationships are the ones most often underdeveloped. When you don't have as much in common and don't appreciate the changing dynamics of risk from personal and functional relationships to those that tend to be more strategic, many underestimate the energy and consciousness required to build these strategic relationships and approach them too simplistically. As such, many U.S. businesspeople are, culturally, underachievers when it comes to building lasting strategic relationships.

Strategic relationships elevate your efforts and thinking beyond your current realm of responsibilities and push you to think about new business opportunities and key stakeholders you'll need to succeed. Strategic relationships transcend time, function, and geographic limitations. They create accelerated access, long-term personal and professional growth opportunities, new market insights, and shed light on *return on influence* versus concerns about corporate politics.

As a first-generation immigrant, I came to this country with $100, a suitcase, and no fluency in the English language. Over the past two decades, I've developed personal, functional, and strategic relationships to build and enhance my career, obtain a Top 10 MBA program

	Personal	Functional	Strategic
Purpose	Enhancing personal and professional development; referral to useful information and contacts	Efficiency Maintain capacity and functions required of the group	Uncovering future challenges and priorities; garnering support of diverse and influential stakeholders
Location and temporal orientation	Mostly externally focused Current and future potential	Mostly internally focused Current demand orientation interests	Internal and externally oriented toward the future
Players and recruitment	Key contacts mostly discretionary Not always clear who is relevant	Key contacts relatively nondiscretionary; prescribed by tasks and org structure; very clear on who's relevant	Key contacts flow from strategic context and the organizational environment; specific membership is discretionary; not always clear who is relevant
Network attributes and key behaviors	Breadth by reaching out to contacts who can make referrals	Depth focused on building working relationships	Leverage by creating hybrid of internal-external connections

education, find valuable suppliers and customers, and complete challenging projects. As an entrepreneur, I've leveraged relationships to raise institutional capital, proactively participate in various mergers and acquisitions, attract and retain global talent, build a multitude of brands, and consult with *Fortune* 500 clients, including KPMG, Inter-Continental Hotels Group, and Siemens.

I know how to strategically quantify business relationships, and so can readers of this pragmatic how-to book of global best practices. But it is critical to point out what this book is *not* about. It's not about networking, using people, how to become more manipulative, how to keep score, or only doing for others if they do for you. It's not about schmoozing, working a room, or using others in general to get what you want. I'm also strenuously against special favoritism, nepotism, cliques, secret societies, and in particular, any efforts perceived as anti-diversity or anti-inclusion. On the contrary, I strongly believe that diversity is more than affirmative action. It is the inclusion of all unique walks of life and experiences, which ultimately delivers a broad-based perspective.

Here's to your strategic relationship success!

1

Why Most "Networking" Doesn't Work!

Today, we are more likely to *call* a colleague who works three offices down the hall from us—or worse yet, *text* her—rather than make the short trip for a face-to-face visit. We pass key team members in our corporate hallways, yet, after having spent the last several months on conference calls, exchanging voicemails and e-mails on key projects, and even seeing them in various company meetings, we have no idea who they are. Who are you e-mailing? Who are you asking for resources? Who are you selling to? Who are you listening to? Who are you asking for help?

When technology, even with its vast operational effectiveness and efficient capabilities, determines the nature of our human interactions, is it any surprise that many believe there has been a dramatic erosion of our sense of community and our ability to touch people? Have we gone so far as to need mandates such as *No E-Mail Fridays?*

In 1916, practical reformer of the Progressive Era and state supervisor of rural schools in West Virginia, L. J. Hanifan, described *social capital* as "Those tangible substances that count for most in the daily lives of people: namely good will, fellowship, sympathy, and social intercourse among the individuals and families who make up a social unit" (*Bowling Alone*, p. 19).

Isn't it interesting that Hanifan's account of social capital anticipated virtually all of the crucial elements in later interpretations of what is essentially the lubricant of our day-to-day interactions as human beings? Unlike the generation before mine, which was proactively involved in various lodges, PTAs, churches, and political parties, I would submit that we are becoming increasingly disconnected as a society in many ways, and even more so in business, where many of us spend the majority of our waking hours.

My intent in the next several chapters is to not only identify a practical and applicable process for identifying, building, nurturing, and leveraging relationships instrumental to your personal and professional success, but also to help *quantify* the economic value of your most valuable and often *strategic* relationships. In short, creation alone won't suffice. Savvy professionals find opportunities to monetize their business relationships through a long-term, mutual *build and benefit* strategy.

Interviewing over 1,000 managers, executives, and directors of emerging growth, middle market, and Fortune 500 client companies has allowed me to identify two schools of thought when it comes to business relationships. On one end of the spectrum is the *art* of building relationships. For many, this is the ability to *engage* others through the exchange of business cards and the building of transactional relationships. There is little to no shortage of resources in the marketplace today to help train and develop those who seem otherwise introverted and must adapt to a social network. Fairly foundational notions such as the elevator pitch, working a room, or learning how to be a conference commando fit into this category. On the other end of the spectrum is the academic world of Social Network Analysis (SNA), or the *science* of relationship building. What began as the study of patterns of human interaction in the 1930s has evolved into a discipline, though often very dry and rather academic.

We believe that Relationship Economics—*the art and science of relationships*—is the hybrid approach necessary for anyone who needs to build and leverage relationships to get things done. Effectiveness and productivity are both measures of outputs, but efficiency also includes the amount of *input* required. Let's start by looking at why most people are inefficient when it comes to business networking and building long-term, value-centric relationships.

Top 10 Reasons Why Networking Doesn't Work

As we talk to companies around the world and work on consulting and training engagements with clients such as KPMG, Inter-Continental Hotels, Disney, Cisco, and Siemens, we have found that one of the consistent reasons people become frustrated with networking is that they don't believe it produces any quantifiable results. Simply put, they don't think much of their effort really works. Whether you are a senior executive, a business unit leader, a project manager, or a salesperson new to a territory, people often forget that their most valuable asset is their portfolio of relationships.

Beyond your educational foundation, experience, wisdom, and all of the skills and talents you have acquired, relationships transcend across geography, function, company, and often any particular point in time.

If you simplify business networking into three stages of preparation, interaction, and follow-through, we have identified the Top 10 culprits that render traditional networking ineffective. They include a lack of purpose or planning, engaging the wrong people or the inability to disengage when necessary, and lastly, the absent notion of triangulation.

Let's take a quick look at each.

In the *preparation* phase, your goals, strategies, and tactics will drive efficiency.

Lack of Purpose

Most people network without a purpose. When they come to me and ask, "Do you know so-and-so?" My first question in response is, "What is your intent or purpose for networking? *Why* do you feel like you need to get to know this person?"

Typically, they don't have a well thought-out answer, or what they do say is often very transactional and based on an immediate need, such as job transition or a prospective client.

Fuzzy Goals

There is no shortage of relationship formulation—many can identify great contacts—but we often struggle with consistent

Relationship-Centric Best Practice: Purpose
Purpose, by the way, has nothing to do with what you do for a living. It is your guiding light and it starts with a healthy self. As my business partner, Jennifer Whitt, likes to say, "If you're not centered—if you don't know who you are, what you stand for, and your true intent for building relationships—how can you genuinely articulate the same to someone else or make course corrections in your efforts along the way?" There is no right or wrong answer here, but it is critical that you start your networking or relationship-building path with an overarching purpose. For example, there is the paternal purpose: *I want to pave an easier path for my children. If I build and nurture key relationships now, it will make it easier for them to get into better schools, land more promising jobs, and have access to a greater wealth of time and opportunities than I did growing up.* This is a purpose that is clearly independent of any particular point in time, geography, or specific functional job.   Others have defined their purpose as emotional discovery or perhaps self-mastery: By getting to know others, I get to know myself better and can grow both personally and professionally.   By starting with a succinct purpose of personal and professional development, building and nurturing productive relationships becomes your compass.

relationship development execution. Goals are the fundamental link to how you translate great ideas into actionable impacts in your life and in your personal and professional relationships.

The notion of business relationships is not a standalone concept. It's an enabler not just toward achieving business goals, but also maximizing an individual, team, and organization's performance, execution, and results. Without succinct, measurable, and success-proof goals, many of your investments in relationship creation will be lost in the nurturing, development, and ultimate capitalization of those relationships. Said another way, you'll spend a lot of time and effort on unproductive coffee shop or lunch visits, and have little to show for that investment of time, effort, or resources.

Are you new to a project team, sales territory, divisional, or leadership role? How will networking help you succeed given the dynamics of your new role? Which relationships will help you enable, accelerate, or maximize your ability to achieve your goals?

By succinctly crafting three to five specific and measurable goals—not just simply self-directed ones such as "becoming a better person," but those that will require collaboration with or cooperation from others, what we refer to as relationship-centric goals—you develop a crystal-clear destination for this desired journey. Many business goals such as attracting and retaining top talent, growing profitable revenues, cost performance, or lasting behavioral changes cannot be achieved in isolation. They require, instead, value-based relationships to accomplish. This is a critical point, as quantifiable relationships must have a barometer against which you can measure your efforts.

You Don't Have a Plan

The bulk of our training and consulting is focused on helping clients link their strategic direction with personal action—how to get good ideas to great execution by leveraging not just the *what* and *how*, but also *with whom*. Your approach to building and nurturing key relationships must be agile, similar to a speedboat, so that if you are not headed in the right direction, you can expeditiously make course corrections.

You simply can't improve what you don't measure. So, if you keep going out and getting involved with organizations and attending networking functions, how are you measuring

> ### Relationship-Centric Best Practice: Vibration versus Forward Motion
>
> It's critical not to confuse vibration with forward motion. Many people equate busy work in networking with progress in relationship creation and capitalization, when in fact it's just that—vibration. Countless meals and coffee visits will seldom turn into newly acquired customers, great employees, or the execution of critical milestones. Unless you have PGP in place, you'll seldom realize the desired forward motion toward achieving critical business goals, objectives, and key strategic initiatives.

the results of that attendance? You constantly meet with the same group of individuals, either inside or outside the organization. Are those investments really producing any meaningful results in your efforts toward reaching your goals and objectives?

One of the fundamental reasons networking doesn't work is that most people network without a plan. They are not methodical, systematic, or disciplined about *which* events they attend, *why* they attend them, *what* they are trying to achieve while there, and *how* they will follow through after the event.

To quickly review, the critical first three areas in which networking fails are *purpose*, *goals*, and *plan*—PGP. This is a great mechanism to consistently think about not only *why* you are building relationships but also *how* you will drive results well beyond any single interaction.

In the *interaction* phase, different situations mandate unique rules of behavior, which will deliver relationship development effectiveness. Networking is not simply a noble cause but rather an endeavor to create preferential advantage. It cannot be left to chance. Here are some common culprits in this phase:

Your Efforts Are Haphazard and Reactive

The process of identifying, building, and nurturing relationships requires disciplined thought and action. In essence, this needs to become the dye in the fabric—not a patch. The dye permeates throughout the fabric. In many ways, the dye *defines* the fabric. A patch is just that—a bandage, a fix, a transaction. If building relationships becomes what you do every day, as opposed to something you feel like you have to do to get by, it tends to become less of an afterthought.

Let me tell you about my first encounter with Joan. It was 6:00 A.M. on a Saturday in May and I was standing in line at a local YMCA, registering my children for upcoming summer programs. Next to me stood an unassuming, five foot tall, middle-aged woman (as she later described herself) wearing no make-up, a T-shirt that should have been donated years ago, black Spandex, and with shuffled registration paperwork spilling from her arms. Curious, I simply began by asking about her children and which programs she was registering them for. As she reciprocated and we got to know each other, I met a giant personality beneath this unpretentious exterior.

Want to know what Joan does for a living? She orchestrates global events for some of the biggest multinational organizations, private conglomerates, industry associations, and nonprofit causes. Her broad sphere of influence extends beyond business contacts to include numerous policy makers and shrewd investors. My question to you is: How many Joans are you walking by every day? How many prospective clients, suppliers, and investors are you choosing to ignore simply because you perceive the circumstances to be inopportune?

Think of the last networking event you attended. A) Most people often have no real resolution or intent as to why they are there. The organization was getting together, so they thought that they should probably show up. (By the way, there is nothing wrong with the innate need to belong. In time, your involvement

> ### Relationship-Centric Best Practice:
> ### An Opportunity Every Minute of Every Day
>
> You have an opportunity to build relationships every minute of every day—both within your organization and outside of it. Unfortunately, people go through most days with their heads buried in their respective checklists, running from one meeting to the next. I equate this to having a lot of machetes, making sure that they are all freshly sharpened and chopping down a lot of trees without ever stopping to ask if you are in the right jungle. "Let's set aside two hours a day to network" is a patch. "I will make time to meet and really get to know a broad array of diverse, interesting people at every opportunity" is the dye. You never know whom you are going to meet at the grocery store, church, or standing in line registering your kids for summer camp. These are but a few opportunities missed every single day by those either too pompous to engage, or simply oblivious to the fact that our lives are all inherently intertwined in a bizarre way. The six-degrees-of-separation cliché is very real.

will provide a multitude of benefits.) B) Most have no idea who else will be at the event and tend to migrate to attendees they already know versus extending or expanding their reach to a broader contact base. And, C) Most are running late from all of the different *have-to* events in their lives, so they show up and get a chance to only grab a quick drink before the program starts. They don't really give themselves an opportunity to engage current and prospective relationships and then end up leaving right afterward to attend yet another commitment.

Sound familiar? If this describes you, then why did you pay the entrance fee and set aside the time to attend the event if you weren't going to be more systematic and disciplined? Are you really starving for more small talk?

Now, consider a different approach to the same networking scenario: First, you prioritize the organizations most relevant to your personal and professional goals and objectives. Many groups plan and publicize their events well in advance, so you aggregate a master list of upcoming events and prioritize your attendance based on those most strategic to your predetermined set of goals, objectives, and action items. You pay and register in advance and place a solid date on your calendar to avoid possible conflicts. Two weeks to a month in advance, you invite a handful of others who you think would also appreciate attending this event. You go online and google the speaker, subject matter of the presentation, or panel discussion so you can arm yourself with insightful perspectives. You show up early, as most events actually have the attendees' name badges at the registration table. You identify three to five people you would like to get to know better and give yourself plenty of time to meet and greet a broad spectrum of attendees. When you meet someone who may not be as engaging or relevant to what you do, you politely disengage.

Time and intellect are your two most valuable assets—you can't afford to waste either. If a conversation is not interesting or productive, you simply must be disciplined enough to move on. Most people get little to no value out of small talk. Instead, ask a poignant question to engage. I'd much rather attend an event and really get to know four or five dynamic, intelligent, interesting, quality people with whom I can follow up after the event instead of going to an event, working the room, and collecting a handful of often useless or irrelevant business cards. Let me save you the time and aggravation: there is something called the Yellow Pages, and it provides the exact same value as the stack of business cards you collected. But if you engage others in meaningful discussions, proactively listen to the content presented, and then have a systematic process to follow through with them afterward, you will have used your time much more fruitfully. Attending events becomes a great deal more relevant if you have thought about your goals, strategies, and tactics in advance.

The other fundamental challenge here is the very reactive nature of most networkers. An example of this is when people are in job transition. What do they do? They network like there is no tomorrow. Their job becomes finding the next job. They ask everyone they meet, *Do you have a job? Do you know someone who has a job?* What typically happens when they find a job? I think we've all seen it. Most stop building those relationships and, worse yet, forget everyone who helped them get there until three years from now, when they call or e-mail you again. One guess as to what they want? That's right—the next job! By establishing this pattern, they build a reputation that says that the only time they call is when they want something versus proactively staying in touch and truly nurturing critical relationships along the way.

Recommended Readings on Social Networking

Years ago, my dad, an avid reader himself, told me: *Leaders are readers and readers are leaders.* I had no fluency in English when I first came to this country and, to this day, still go through the painstaking process of constantly looking up definitions and synonyms to grasp a contextual understanding of the broader content. Through this practice, I have managed to develop a passion for not only absorbing interesting content, but also really thinking through its applications in my life.

In my keynote speeches as well as in this book, I highlight many influential works. At any given point of time, I am often reading four or five books on a variety of topics. Instead of aimless music or obnoxious radio talk shows, I prefer books on tape, CDs, or insightful podcasts from a dozen or so mentors on my iPod. Having read 100-plus books on the topic of social networks, my suggested readings follow. Most are available on the authors' respective web sites.

- Baker, Wayne
  - *Achieving Success Through Social Capital: Tapping Hidden Resources in Your Personal and Business Networks*
  - *Social Networks and Loss of Capital*
  - *Positive Organizational Network Analysis and Energizing Relationships*
  - *Enabling Positive Social Capital in Organizations*
- Beckstrom, Rod and Brafman, Ori
  - *The Starfish and the Spider: The Unstoppable Power of Leaderless Organizations*
- Burt, Ron
  - *Brokerage and Closure*
  - *Teaching Executives to See Social Capital: Results from a Field Experiment*
  - *Network Duality of Social Capital*
  - *Gossip and Reputation*
- Cialdini, Robert
  - *Influence: The Psychology of Persuasion*
  - *The Practice of Social Influence in Multiple Cultures*
  - *Training in Ethical Influence*
- Cohen, Don and Prusak, Laurence
  - *In Good Company: How Social Capital Makes Organizations Work*
- Covey, Stephen M. R.
  - *The Speed of Trust: The One Thing That Changes Everything*

(continued)

Recommended Readings on Social Networking (Continued)

- Gladwell, Malcolm
  - *Blink: The Power of Thinking Without Thinking*
  - *The Tipping Point: How Little Things Can Make a Big Difference*
- Putnam, Robert
  - *Bowling Alone: The Collapse and Revival of American Community*
- Rosen, Emanuel
  - *Buzz: Accelerating Natural Contagion*
  - *The Anatomy of Buzz: How to Create Word of Mouth Marketing*
- Watts, Duncan
  - *Six Degrees: The Science of a Connected Age*
  - *Small Worlds: The Dynamics of Networks Between Order and Randomness*

I'm often reminded of Harvey Mackay's book, *Dig Your Well Before You're Thirsty*. You have to build and nurture these relationships well before you need them. People are a lot less likely to respond and react if you only call when you want something instead of getting in touch to find out how they are doing and how you can become an asset to them. (See the section on *relationship givers, takers, and investors* later in this chapter.)

When I hear someone say, "I *need* to network," that sounds desperate. That's *reactive*. They are looking for a job or they are behind in their sales quota and are scrambling to find prospects, or they are in trouble with their project deliverables. Success comes from being much more proactive. I recently had a chance to meet Keith Ferrazzi of *Never Eat Alone* fame, and I appreciate his advice in the book to keep your calendar full of opportunities to meet and engage a diverse portfolio of contacts.

I liken this kind of networking to playing a game of chess. What I love about playing chess is that it forces you to proactively think a number of moves ahead. Similar to what I understand of military situations, it also challenges you to constantly conduct situational analysis. Where am I today, what am I trying to achieve, what happens if I make these efforts, and what's next? Investing in your relationships is also a constant situational analysis. It's critical to think about relationships as investments, and like any other investment, it's imperative to evaluate your return on that investment. When it comes to relationships, ROI needs to be reinvented. Think about this in regard to your *Return on Involvement*. You belong to all of these different organizations and attend all of these functions. What do you have to show for it? Later in this book, we'll discuss *Return on Integration, Return on Impact, Return on Influence*, and *Return on Image*—all quantifiable perspectives on investments in a critical soft asset: your relationships.

What's In It For Me (WIIFM)?

You have to find ways to invest in others or make *relationship currency* deposits, as I cover in later chapters. Find ways to become an asset to others and in quantifiable measures, add value to their efforts. Those who understand the true *value* of a relationship will find a way to reciprocate—maybe not today, tomorrow, or this year, but reciprocity is a natural and undisputable law in the *favor economy*.

Unfortunately, many people overlook the critical nature of such reciprocity in favor of focusing solely on their own situation. Another observation that I've made at many functions has been the perpetual nature of many to think, *What's in it for me?* In essence, they attend functions with their hand out. To recipients of this posture, the interaction becomes a complete turnoff, as it is perceived to be insincere and self-serving. Questions that should be conversational come across as an interrogation, and the person probing often asks intimate questions about information most people are not comfortable sharing with someone that they met just 15 seconds before. Their comments come across as scripted or somehow manufactured. They are, in essence, *harvesting conversations*.

Compare and contrast this approach with the one that we coach participants in our workshops to use, which involves investing most of their efforts in engaging the other person to really understand what they are about. Take the time to understand their issues and challenges, and give them a reason to want to get to know you better. If you add value to every conversation with a unique perspective, the comment you most often tend to hear is, "Wow, I never thought of it that way." And the perception becomes one of continued interest for a follow-up dialogue.

Relationship-Centric Best Practice: Asking Better Questions

If you want better answers, ask better questions! Alan Weiss often comments: "Ask engaging questions and you'll influence the conversation. Influence the conversation and you'll influence the relationship. Influence the relationship and you'll influence the outcome you desire." What engaging questions are *you* asking to influence your conversations and key relationships?

INSTEAD OF ASKING:	TRY ASKING:
What do you do?	How are you measured?
Are people *really* your biggest asset?	Where would developing intracompany relationships rank in your performance evaluation plan?

Do your people know how to collaborate?	Do you have teams or committees?
How effective is your formal mentoring program?	Have you thought about reverse mentoring?
Tell me about your talent acquisition efforts.	Tell me about your fear of flight risk.

When I meet an executive or individual for the first time, I'm not gauging whether we can do business together, whether we can do a project together, or whether he can help me. Instead, I'm assessing, *Does this person understand and value relationships?* And if I start by making a deposit—by finding a way to become an asset in solving their challenges—will he find a way to reciprocate? It is important to point out that I am not talking about only doing for others who are going to do for you, but as we all know, it is a lot easier to ask for a withdrawal *after* you have made a deposit.

According to the psychological perspective of former PepsiCo, Lucent, and HP human resources executive and friend, Pat Dailey, Ph.D., "establishing relationships is a process of successive disclosures. You give me a little of you, I take it and make a judgment. I give you a little of me, you absorb it and make a judgment." This evolutionary process comes to fruition faster for those with the DNA to process the give and take more quickly. However, you certainly don't have to be slick and quick to become an efficient relationship builder. In our experience, everyone has a unique pace in mastering these skills and behaviors and it is critical to clearly understand the line of too much, too fast in the early stages of relationship formation.

Every job has its issues and challenges. At the next networking function, start by asking people how you can be an asset to them. Think about who you know that can help them and how you can make an impactful deposit for this person.

I have a personal three-touch rule that I follow. I will make three investments without expecting anything in return.

As I meet individuals who are looking for knowledge, talent, or an introduction to an influential relationship, I'll go out of my way to somehow become an asset to them. But the fundamental challenge is that you simply don't have enough bandwidth to invest in all of your relationships equally. How you prioritize which relationships you invest in has to be congruent with your relationship-centric goals and objectives and your individual definition for a return on your relationship investments.

Everyone is tuned in to the same FM station—WIIFM. What's In It For Me. The next time you meet someone, instead of having your hand out and wondering what she can do for you, *lend* a hand by asking, "How can I *really* get to know this person and find ways to become an asset to *her?* How can I find ways to create *quantifiable value* for her?"

Relationship Economics @ Work:
Bob McIntosh at Rock-Tenn Company

When Bob McIntosh, senior VP and general counsel for Rock-Tenn Company, is evaluating potential service providers, competency, service level, and expense are at the top of his evaluation list. But relationships are also an important factor.

"Performance comes first," he said. "But relationships absolutely come into play. Take investment bankers, for example. These are very large firms that often service a particular industry. They are in the business. They are selling their services, but as a potential buyer, you also want an investment banker who will bring you deal flow when they come across an opportunity."

Rock-Tenn's corporate strategy includes organic growth plans, as well as some inorganic opportunities, Bob said. These strategies are transparent to bankers, who are aware of the kinds of acquisitions the firm is interested in.

On a regular basis, investment banking firms who want to do business with Rock-Tenn will visit and share ideas about potential transactions that might interest the firm. This includes companies (or divisions of companies) that may be available for purchase.

"They may bring it up to gauge our interest," said Bob. "Of course, the hope is that they build a relationship with us so that when a deal comes up that we're interested in because it is a quality deal that fits within our growth strategy, we'll choose them as the investment bank that assists us with the deal."

Wrong People

Some of my favorite networking functions are early morning breakfast briefings. I am an early bird and most attendees have yet to face the minutia of the day, so they are likely to attend for the two critical factors: content and community.

I recently attended a Harvard Business School executive breakfast series held at the Buckhead Club in Atlanta, which featured Mark Fields, president of the Americas for the Ford Motor Company. It doesn't get much better than this. The content was interesting, and so was the caliber of the people both anticipated and found in attendance. Doors typically open at 7:30 A.M. with the program starting around 8:00, and wrapping up by 9:00. I was simply amazed by the number of people who showed up after the program began and completely missed the opportunity to engage the attendees in advance of the content. Conversely, those who were prompt, if not early, had the opportunity to connect with some of the sharpest minds in the local business, political, and philanthropic communities.

Even at events with great opportunities such as this one, you tend to have those in attendance who, although polite and cordial, are not relevant to your current role, realm of responsibilities, or aspirations. Let's just call one of these people "Steve." He's a poultry expert in a very obscure agricultural field that has little to no relevance within my current intellectual radar. After a few minutes, I quickly gauged that not only did Steve and I have little in common personally, but I could find little value to add to his efforts. Similarly, he brought few insights or knowledge of the types of clients that my business serves. I thanked Steve for his time and simply mentioned the need to say hello to a few others at the event.

The number one mistake most people make when they walk into an event like this one is that they spend the entire 30 to 45 minutes talking to someone who is not relevant to what they are doing, and they get sidetracked from their game plan. When I refer to the "wrong people," it is not intended to mean that some people have less value than others. I am simply trying to get you focused on *relevancy*. How relevant is this individual to the goals and objectives that you are trying to achieve? Please understand that this comment is not to be construed as manipulative. It's not about an elegant way of using people, but about being smarter about how you invest your valuable time, efforts, and resources.

One of the best practices in this section is to identify what we call influential hubs. These are subject matter experts or those naturally highly connected who are consistently able to engage and influence others over a certain period of time. If you think of the classic bike wheel, they represent the hub in the middle with the many spokes fanning out from that position.

Certain functional roles lend themselves naturally well to this concept. The best commercial real estate agents I know are very well connected in their communities to a multitude of possible direct client or referral sources. The best attorneys, accountants, insurance agents, recruiters, nonprofit fundraisers, lobbyists, and industry consultants are often very good hubs because of the diversity of friendships that they build over the years. It is critical to your relationship-building approach to identify those hubs and find ways to become an asset to them.

Remember that one of the fastest ways to turn off a hub is to go to that person and say, "What can you do for me?" Though these hubs are typically genuine and go out of their way to help

Relationship Economics @ Work:
Dan Brown and Heavy Hitters at Various Functions

According to Dan Brown, a personal friend and former executive at SunTrust Bank, "It all starts with relationship building. You have to find some common ground with whomever you are dealing. You can't be too needy—it has to be a relationship of equals. This begins with a centered self. If I am at an interesting function and there are some heavy hitters there, I don't necessarily have to approach them. If I am there having conversations with a group of people, some of these heavy hitters might come up to me and introduce themselves."

So I asked Dan, how does he characterize a *heavy hitter*? "This is someone in a relationship-type area who deals with a lot of people, travels globally; they're often an expert in their respective field—someone who if you are in that function, are [sic] deemed very influential."

What makes some of these hubs more attractive than others? "It largely depends on the function and the person. There is the internal persona and then the function that they play. Some people are heavy hitters internally—no matter where they are, they are people you want to know. Others have a heavy hitting function, but they are not necessarily someone you care to spend any time with. Others, no matter what position they are in, they are an interesting person to get to know.

"Where do I spend my time? Sometimes you just spend time with people who [sic] you find interesting, not necessarily someone whose role can benefit you."

Dan and I have been involved in the High Tech Ministries Prayer Breakfast for years, thanks to another personal friend and mentor, Charlie Paparelli. In many ways, Dan was instrumental in helping me focus my avocation as my

(continued)

Relationship Economics @ Work: Dan Brown and Heavy Hitters at Various Functions (Continued)

vocation. Six years ago, over a cup of coffee, he mentioned that I networked better than anyone else he had ever met and wondered if I would come to his church and speak about my approach to building and nurturing relationships.

Assuming there would be a dozen or so attendees, I prepared a few remarks only to find myself in an auditorium in front of 250-plus audience members. After a 45-minute speech, I stayed for 90 minutes afterward to answer individual questions and share best practices. From that one session, I was invited to speak to 30 other similar gatherings at other churches, Rotary and academic groups, which led to keynote speeches at corporate and association clients and the journey which has become our firm today. Dan remains a great personal friend and is now an interim executive on various operations and strategic technology assignments.

people, you will quickly brand yourself a taker by approaching them in this way. What is critical to hubs, or to any relationship development effort, is that you truly invest time, effort, and resources in advancing the achievement of others.

During the *follow-through* phase, systematic, disciplined thought and action will drive recognition. If you believe in the premise that most people genuinely want to help, then it becomes incumbent upon you to not just follow up (transactional), but follow through (transformational) the initial success in meeting and engaging interesting, relevant contacts.

Arming Others with Ammunition

When people say that networking doesn't work, they usually cite as evidence the fact that they have invested in others in the past without any reciprocity from the other side. When I inquire specifically, *How did you arm them with the appropriate context to introduce or recommend you?* The answer is often a blank stare.

We can easily distinguish between the "Joe Blank" approach of looking for a handout, versus Keith Conley's style of trying to figure out a way to become an asset in the best practice that follows. In this process, if you can get to know me, understand my business, and what my challenges are, you can uncover ways to help me. And when you do, my next logical question will be how

---

Business Relationship *Don'ts*: "John Nobody Sent Me!"

I recently received a voicemail to the effect of: "David, this is Joe Blank, friend of John Nobody *(whose name I honestly did not recognize at first and later recalled that I didn't care for him at all)*. I was wondering if you could meet me on XYZ dates and times and let me pick your brain for some of your contacts in my current job search. John says you know everyone in town." You can't make this stuff up.

I continue to wonder, *What was he thinking?* What in that voicemail could possibly propel me to take action? Nonetheless, acting on a favorite grandmother's advice to always be nice, I return Joe Blank's call to inquire about his job search. "Well, I'm looking for a VP of sales role," he declares. "I have been selling for 40-plus years and can't possibly imagine a job out there that I couldn't do."

I asked him about possible target industries, size, or types of companies, or relevant background and applicable strengths. With each of these inquiries, I consistently felt that he was making me draw this information out of him.

Because Joe Blank was not forthcoming in discussing his situation, I wasn't able to help him in the manner that he had hoped. He essentially wanted the return on his investment—without having to make any investment.

---

can *I* help *you*. That's when you can tell me that you are in transition and looking for a VP of sales position.

Relationship Economics @ Work: Keith Conley on Credibility by Association

I was introduced to the head of the professional services group at NCR, Keith Conley, through Scott Jones, a friend at IBM Global Services. Not only did Scott's introduction of Keith provide the credibility by association, but it was also done in person with a high degree of touch and care. Keith was well prepared, having viewed my background online, and presented me with a polished background and bio, as well as a highly customized personal marketing plan outlining specific organizations, contacts, and roles he would most like to pursue. After an extremely productive visit, he followed through with an introductory paragraph, soft copies of his resume and credentials, and a summary of contacts to whom I had offered to introduce him.

Another fundamental best practice further discussed in this book was Keith's innate ability to gauge my interest in the relationship and the immediate added value he could bring from our continued interactions.

Most people have way too much on their plates to go through the Spanish Inquisition—especially when they are looking for help. A much easier and more effective approach is the example of Keith's efforts and an offer to briefly visit and uncover specific opportunities of how you can be an asset to one another.

Create a one-page marketing profile that explains your background, past industries in which you have worked, and whatever your specific differentiators may be. This gives other people a snapshot of who you are and gets them thinking about who they know who could be an asset to you.

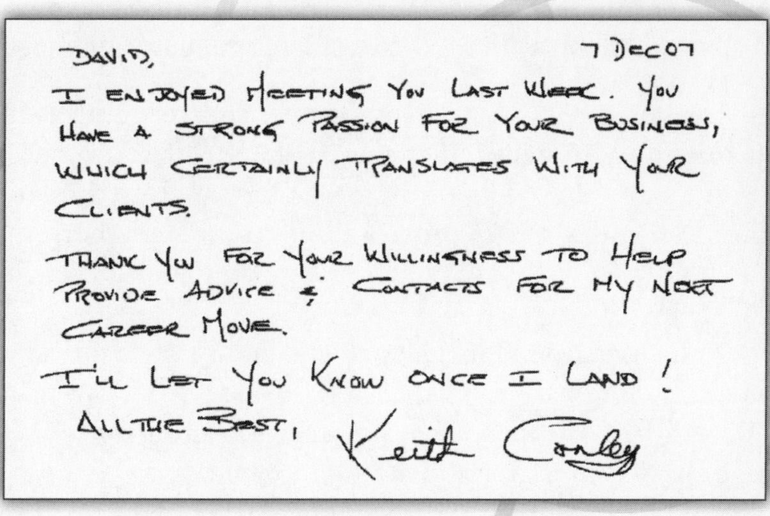

DAVID, 7 DEC 07

I ENJOYED MEETING YOU LAST WEEK. YOU HAVE A STRONG PASSION FOR YOUR BUSINESS, WHICH CERTAINLY TRANSLATES WITH YOUR CLIENTS.

THANK YOU FOR YOUR WILLINGNESS TO HELP PROVIDE ADVICE & CONTACTS FOR MY NEXT CAREER MOVE.

I'LL LET YOU KNOW ONCE I LAND!

ALL THE BEST,
Keith Conley

FIGURE 1.1 Highly Personalized Post-Introductory Note.

Arm people with the appropriate information they need to help you. It is critical not to leave this to chance. Come to the table prepared with a systematic game plan that explains how we can become an asset to each other!

Personal handwritten notes such as the one in Figure 1.1 from Keith Conley elevate you above the market noise.

Relationship Economics @ Work: Pat Dailey on Becoming an Asset and Arming with Success-Proof Information

I met Pat Dailey several years ago when he was in career transition. Pat is a global HR leader who is passionate in the recruitment and integration of senior teams around the globe. As I got to know him, I learned that he is fundamentally an architect of employer-of-choice practices that attract top-tier talent. With each interaction, he clearly demonstrates deep expertise in transforming organizations challenged by strategic repositioning, globalization,

(*continued*)

Relationship Economics @ Work: Pat Dailey on Becoming an Asset and Arming with Success-Proof Information (Continued)

turnarounds, SG&A cost reductions, and reengineering. Working in a function that many believe is purely focused on the tactical aspects of the role, Pat is a clear-thinking business leader with a proven ability to upgrade both the credibility as well as the quantifiable contribution of the HR team.

His background includes chief administrative officer at Herbalife International, VP of global workforce management at HP, VP of HR for the network products group of Alcatel-Lucent, VP of HR for Banc One Services Corp., now a division of JPMorgan Chase, and a partner at Korn/Ferry International. Performance clearly trumps all, but beyond that, as we got to know each other, Pat has always offered to be an asset. In an effort to reciprocate his kindness, I offered to introduce him to a number of private equity relationships. What follows is an example of the information with which he armed me to not only make that offer more successful (After all, who best to present your credentials than you?), but to mitigate the risk of me formulating his credentials to chance.

Subject: Virtual Intro: Pat Daily—PepsiCo-trained Senior HR Executive

Neal—I had a good lunch visit with David today and he asked about the progress of our discussions, so I wanted to touch base to see if you've thought any further about getting the portfolio execs together in 2008. I will also call you early next week to follow up.

Separately, I want to introduce you and Steve to Patrick Dailey. Pat is targeting his search for a number one HR role—most likely with a company navigating business transformation and proactively upgrading its competitive capability. His geography is wide open and his hands-on expertise includes best practices at companies such as PepsiCo, Hewlett-Packard, and the U.K.-based BOC Group.

Pat is a leader with distinctive experience including:

- *Chief Talent Scout.* Recruiting, assessing talent, and assembling senior leadership teams, globally
- *Changing the DNA.* Leading and partnering a range of organizational transformation and performance initiatives
- *Succession Planning.* Developing the leadership pipeline and orchestrating leadership change with continuity
- *Board of Director Experience.* BOD Selection. Installing *performance-based* executive compensation plans
- *High-Performance Culture.* Building sustainable cultures and reward systems that guide and retain great talent
- *Protecting the Corporation.* Managing and monitoring SOX and Code of Conduct compliance and
- *Global HR Leadership.* Inspiring and coaching a lean, global HR team within a highly matrixed organization.

I can answer questions you might have about Pat but please feel free to contact him directly at XXX. His CV is also attached.

Best,

David Nour

Ideal Relationship Profiles

There are many social networking tools in the market today to help you find specific contacts. Some of the better ones I've found include LinkedIn, ZoomInfo, Spoke, and Plaxo. All of these tools enable you to identify contacts. The web site theyrule .net, for example, will show you who is on whose board and profiles these key individuals.

Type *Equifax*, one of the credit-reporting companies, based here in Atlanta, into ZoomInfo and you will see that Rick Smith, the current CEO, came to the company follow

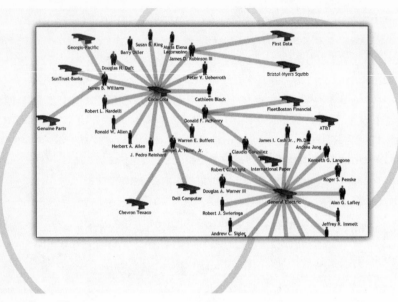

FIGURE 1.2   TheyRule.net Board-Level Social Network.

22 years at GE. ZoomInfo not only shows you Rick's background and tells you that he is on the board of directors of the Commerce Club, attended Purdue University, and his previous roles at GE, but it also shows you a picture of the Equifax board and provides you with their respective profiles. (See Chapter 10 for an in-depth review of the most prevalent social networking technologies in the market today.) Figure 1.2 is one such tool from TheyRule.net.

There is a plethora of publicly available information out there to help you profile key individuals who could be instrumental to your success. This independent due diligence prepares you for an insightful interaction, with intelligent remarks about the company or its leadership, and greater opportunities to work with Rick and his team in addressing critical company challenges and opportunities.

Other popular tools here include Hoovers, OneSource, Factiva, BusinessWise, and Leadership Library. There is certainly no shortage of resources for exceptional due diligence information to profile key individuals that are instrumental to your success. Most of these sites are limited to the more visible roles—mainly executives—but with Google, it is very difficult for any of us to hide. So if the individual you are trying to meet has ever written an article, been published, or spoken at an event, chances are that his profile, background, and points of interest are going to be online. I have also found *McKinsey Quarterly*, Booz Allen's *strategy + business*, and CEOExpress.com to be invaluable tools.

Absent Notion of Triangulation

Another common mistake in most people's relationship-building efforts is that they do not verify, validate, or void the critical assumptions that they make. You don't want to walk into a meeting, or any situation, with mis- or outdated information.

I'm embarrassed to admit that during a recent visit with a couple of executives at McKesson, I was politely taken aside and coached that the executive who referred me to them did not leave under the best circumstances and that the mention of his name in the future could be detrimental to my efforts.

So that they don't find themselves in similar situations, we coach clients to do what we call *triangulation*. (See Figure 1.3.)

Identify two or three independent sources who have a vested interest in gaining access or working with the same individual that you do. Double-check your information and the key assumptions that you're making about your relationship-development efforts. Is this person still in charge of this project? Is this person responsible for this engagement? Is this person physically based out of this office? I have heard nightmare stories of people getting on a plane for a meeting in New York only to find that the person they are meeting with changed jobs recently and is completely irrelevant to the critical opportunities at hand.

Triangulate realms of responsibilities. What is this person's real clout? What projects is he involved in? How many people

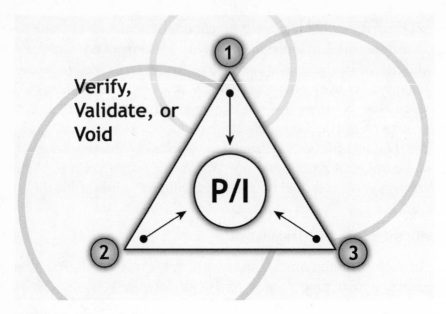

FIGURE 1.3 Triangulation.

are on this person's team? If this relationship is important to you, it is critical to do some research in advance to find other trusted sources that this individual works with.

A recent survey polled 100,000 executives about the best way to create access both inside and outside the organization. The overwhelming response—over 85 percent—was "through a trusted source." That source could be a very viable lieutenant who works with them and knows you and can recommend you, or it can be an outside adviser such as an accountant, lawyer, or consultant whom this individual has worked with who can likewise recommend you. Triangulation and the KEI map I wrote about earlier also help you understand who a firm's trusted sources are. Who are their advisers? Who works with them, in what capacity, and how can you become an asset to them? Knowing this enables you to more effectively customize your presentation and add value to the individual with whom you are trying to work.

Givers, Takers, and Investors

In my experience, there are three types of networkers: Givers (God bless Mother Teresa), Takers (we've all known some), and Investors. Which one are you? If I asked your colleagues and your friends, which would *they* say that you are?

As I have mentioned before, some people only reach out to you when they want something. I call those people *takers*. They have a very "me centric" approach to their networking. I am not sure I would even call what they form *relationships* because their transactional network and contacts are made solely for their benefit—and only *their* benefit.

Business Relationship *Don'ts*: "Drive-By Greetings"

I'm an adviser to the DBM International Center for Executive Options (ICEO). Here in Atlanta, Jim Deupree and Bob Chaet do a great job coaching senior executives in transition to appropriately aim their compass toward an opportunity they'd be most passionate about in the next chapter of their careers. Unfortunately, having had the rug pulled out from under them (often through no fault of their own) most of these execs typically network like mad to uncover that next job. They fill their calendars with endless coffee meetings, countless e-mail touches, and a myriad of "networking events." They proactively reach out to everyone they used to live next to, go to school with, work with, play with, and even parents of their kids' soccer teammates. They really work it.

Until they find a job. Then, not only do they stop the activity and tend to go dark under the new rug (which will get pulled out from under them in another few years), but much more detrimentally, they forget the amazing alumni of friends and colleagues, advisers, and hubs who helped them

(continued)

Business Relationship *Don'ts*:
"Drive-By Greetings" (Continued)

in the process. Other colleagues who are likewise in search of their next opportunity are suddenly forgotten. Favors promised are ignored. And catch-up visits with those still in the market become less important than that corporate visit.

Instead of embracing the very portfolio of relationships that enabled their success, these people further distance themselves. Until three years down the road, when they come looking for another job. How likely are you to help them? Most are not. I actually call them on it and outright ask, "When was the last time you called to see how *I* am doing and how *my* business has been since your last search?"

However, the altruistic givers are just as bad. Don't get me wrong—there is a certain nobility in being the Mother Teresa of relationship giving. All this crowd does is give. They are driven by doing for others, but they become sheepish when *they* need help.

Patricia, who is a good friend of mine here in Atlanta, is directly responsible for a great number of CIOs having found their current roles. Yet, when she could have used their help for a charity fundraising event, an incredibly worthy cause, for whatever reason, she was reluctant to seek their support.

What Patricia and all the other givers must realize is that when you give, you are making deposits—by doing for others—and those investments are perishable. You will lose on the opportunity to leverage those relationships and therefore will have zero to show for all of that generosity, other than self-gratification. It is critical to point out here that we are not talking about keeping score or only doing for others who do for you. But as with most things in life, too much of either of these—taking or giving—will fail to benefit you in any way. You must find an appropriate middle ground on which to form personal connections.

The savvy professional is a relationship investor. These are the people who understand that you have to start by giving. You have to make an investment to get a return on that investment.

Long before a need to capitalize or monetize relationships, an investor has accumulated a great deal of social capital through the development of a strong *Relationship Bank*. His name alone creates a sense of obligation to deliver value. Said another way, these are the people you would bend over backward to help, not only because they have gone out of their way to help you in the past, but because whenever you need help, they embrace you with open arms.

Similar to any other investments, relationship investors read their prospectus. They truly consider their portfolio of relationships to be their biggest asset and constantly aim to analyze and enhance their return on relationship investments. In Chapter 3, I discuss *Strategic Relationship Planning* best practices.

No one has enough resources to invest in every relationship equally, so you must prioritize your relationships and decide which to invest in more. This is not to say that you should be anything less than cordial and gracious in meeting and engaging others. But you also have to make sure they understand that true relationships are reciprocal in nature and investments made in building and nurturing relationships must be realized as a value-add at some future time.

Corporate Relationship Deficit Disorder

Business relationships are formed in a variety of contexts. One of the misconceptions of business relationships is that they are purely an external asset or liability. But a great deal of our work over the last several years has been focused on intracompany relationships.

Companies, regardless of size or industry and despite efforts to the contrary by their leadership, tend to build geographic, functional, and project-based silos. Have you ever heard the ongoing disputes between the Los Angeles and New York offices, for example? By definition, those geographies will compete for mind share and wallet share of the corporate headquarters and often create geographic silos.

Likewise, when most organizations are structured by functional capabilities—whether they are practice groups in a law firm or finance, engineering, marketing, and legal within most corporations—they are forced to compete for resources. Doesn't that create functional silos?

Lastly, if key initiatives tend to be organized by cross-geography and cross-functional projects, isn't that project team often competing for access, influence, and resources? As such, aren't project-based silos not only created, but often nurtured in time? Many corporations, because of their sheer structure, performance expectations, measurements, and rewards, are not conducive to collaboration and not constructed for communication, and what suffers most are the intracompany relationships. And just like a family, when it is broken on the inside, guess who sees it.

Cultural Divide

An obsession with transactions first and relationships later often tends to distance us from other people instrumental to our personal and professional success. Many have heard of the socio- and certainly the economic divide. In more recent years, we have also heard of the digital divide. But I would submit that the cultural divide in our global economy is the biggest culprit in hindering the development and nurturing of both intra- as well as externally focused relationships.

Travel to the kingdom of Bahrain and you'll see that a business transaction often includes not only personal embraces, but a predominant focus on character—in essence, more emphasis on the DNA of the individual, and considerably less on the transaction. On a recent trip to the Middle East, I met Basim Al Saie,

managing director of Installux-Golf, and Fasil Ali Reza, managing director of Ali Reza and Sons. They represent an infectious
level of patriotism and all that is right and good about the Arab
world. These highly U.S.-educated (both went to school in Boston), affluent, family-centric business executives see more in an
individual's character than they do the value of a transaction. As a
matter of fact, much of the world comes to the United States and
is surprised, if not offended, by our unquenchable thirst for
transaction success before we show any signs of a personal
connection.

Relationship-Centric Best Practice: Welcoming More than just the Employee

Think about it: the last time Michael and his entire family
were transferred from San Diego to Chicago, his immediate
manager barely got out an e-mail on the Friday afternoon
before that Michael would be joining the team the next
Monday. Why not organize a small reception at the manager's home, invite key employees and their spouses, Michael
and his wife, Lori, and make it a personal mission to make
sure they feel comfortable in their new personal and professional surroundings? Because despite popular belief, I
would submit that: A) what Michael does for a living isn't
who Michael is, and B) if Lori doesn't feel at home in
Chicago, the stay for the job will be a short-term transaction rather than a long-term investment in the position of
the company.

2

The Evolution of Quantifiable Relationships

I t has been said that knowledgeable people know a lot of facts. They know a lot of information. Successful and prosperous ones know a lot of people. They realize that relationships are their most valuable asset and they consistently, intentionally, systematically, and thus strategically nurture those relationships. Ask yourself, how many respected, trusted, influential executives with decision-making ability and real access to power from your list of contacts do you play golf with every week? How many would return your calls and e-mails within 24 hours? How many would come to your support when called upon in a time of need? In short, do you have *contacts* or do you have *relationships?*

Many organizations have become fairly astute in the measurement and analysis of their hard assets such as inventory, cost of goods sold, and return on equity (ROE). The next evolution is measuring, analyzing, and capitalizing on their soft assets, including brands, people, and relationships. This chapter highlights the quantifiable value of each of these soft assets, and challenges—perhaps even reinvents—the traditional understanding of ROI (Return on Investment) with that of *Return on Influence. Return on Involvement. Return on Integration. Return on Impact.* And *Return on Image.*

Measuring and Leveraging Organizational Soft Assets

Most organizations clearly understand hard assets such as inventory and real estate and often characterize them as a barometer by which the company's financial stability and capacity for leverage are measured.

Soft assets are characterized as intangible and tend to be more nebulous. Savvy organizations have in recent years identified and accounted for their unique and inherent value. They include such line items as brand equity, human capital, and strategic relationships—perhaps identified as alliances, joint ventures, or long-term customer or supplier contracts. Although they may not appear on most financial reports, they are proving to be unique, sustainable competitive differentiators and a certain barrier to entry for others.

Brand Equity

Brand equity is certainly an accepted and highly valued soft asset. Take SBC Communications' acquisition of AT&T, for example. The name of the new entity is AT&T, after a global study indicated that it is one of the most recognized brands in the world. Or consider global companies such as GE, Siemens, and Honeywell, which are willing to pay hundreds of millions of dollars in naming rights to align themselves with the Disney brand.

Coca-Cola's estimated brand equity is close to $80 billion. Arguably the most successful product in the history of commerce and certainly the world's most recognized soft drink, Coke has truly become a timeless symbol of authenticity, original, and "real" refreshment. Great brands create the air cover of awareness, instant desirability, and ultimately, loyalty and repeat business beyond the initial trial.

It has been said that it is cheaper to innovate than to advertise. Innovation, prestige, and the consistent ability to elevate themselves above the market noise has propelled many brands into the vocabulary of our daily communications. *FedEx this. Amex that. Do you have a Band-Aid? Can I get a Coke?* And in more recent years, *Let's eBay it, Skype me,* or *Let's get LinkedIn.*

I recently heard John Hackett, CMO of Coca-Cola North America, speak about the critical components in brand communications, including:

- *Positioning*, which is stable over time (Volvo and safety, Crest and cavity fighting)

- *Idea,* that which occupies the emotional space with consumer and cultural insights (Apple and creativity, Harley Davidson and freedom)
- *Creativity,* defined as inspiration as well as inspiring a sphere of influence (Godiva, the "sweet with a dark side")
- *Voice,* which is the emotional relationship with consumers (De Beers—A diamond is forever)

Great brands build a consistent relationship with a multitude of constituents, often with unique requirements at critical points along a very similar desired journey—one of predictability, consistency, and lasting value beyond an economic cycle. Strategic business relationships inside as well as outside an organization not only demand the same predictability, consistency, and lasting value, but also require the same level of investment many organizations make in their brand equity.

Human Capital and the Global War for Talent

Beyond the current global war on terror, there is a global war for talent. This is the reason why sales managers aggressively recruit sales reps with a strong Rolodex, and why acquiring companies are willing to pay handsome multiples for mind share and wallet share growth. A recent Association for Corporate Growth (ACG) Thompson survey attributed the number one reason for the flurry of recent merger and acquisition activity as one of profitable revenue growth—driven by internal as well as externally focused *relationships*.

As evidenced by popular books such as *Topgrading*, the war for talent has been defined as a strategic business initiative and critical enabler of corporate execution. It also happens to be the absolute top challenge in hypergrowth markets such as China and the Gulf Cooperation Council (GCC), a trade bloc involving the six Arab states of the Persian Gulf. Every organization has an ongoing need to assess its current, as well as growth-centric talent requirements. Because of enduring economic and social forces and the struggle to keep top-notch talent in critical roles, this trend is likely to continue for the next several years. A successful campaign in this war requires more than just assertive and creative recruiting. Another critical attribute is a relationship-centric culture with a systematic, disciplined process to retain, develop, and constantly challenge high-performing teams. Countless studies centered on the cost of a bad hire continue to reiterate the critical nature of succinctly identifying this process, as well as executing it with vigor and consistency.

Relationship-Centric Best Practice: Blue Print for High-Performing Teams

According to the *Journal of Applied Psychology*, high-performing employees have a 40 percent to 80 percent greater positive impact on firm performance than average employees. Based on our research, what follows are the 30 critical attributes of highly dynamic, relationship-centric, high-performing teams. There are three categories split between individual competencies (self-motivating and self-correcting), team dynamics (competent and credible), and the relationship-centric organization (decentralized and adaptive).

INDIVIDUAL COMPETENCIES	TEAM DYNAMICS	RELATIONSHIP-CENTRIC ORGANIZATIONS
• *Competitive*—prioritizes external targets and threats, willing and able to compete and win	• *Competent*—very well skilled, well practiced; mastery of communication and inner dependencies	• *Adaptive*—consistently scans the periphery to learn and navigate change with confidence and agility

- *Connected*—proactively creates and capitalizes quantifiable and strategic relationships at the edges of the organization
- *Candid*—exhibits the courage to oppose the status quo

- *Committed*— emotionally engaged and dedicated to targets and values; very high degree of loyalty
- *Coalition*—builds cross-functional or business influence and respect; collaborates and delivers on commitments; incredibly dependable

- *Big Thinking*— innovates by doing differently versus incrementally

- *Emotionally Astute*— deep sense of allegiance with multigenerational workforce

- *Gives Credit*—credits contributions, successes, and ideas of others

- *Conflict as an Asset*—a constructive approach to resolving dysfunctional team dynamics

- *Execution*—speed, accuracy, precision, solid insights

- *Asks for Help*—seeks support of others for supplemental, clarifying information

- *Feedback Loop*—high degree of *measure, analyze,* and *enhance* processes

- *Follow-through*— memory and delivery of commitments made by senior leadership

- *Engaging*—uses facts and convictions to persuade with the unique ability to frame, explain and defend

- *Peer Discipline*—self-governance of performance expectations

- *Keeps it Simple*— consistently transforms metrics and processes into boiled-down, simple, clear, and succinct elements

- *Compliant*—operates within legal and ethical guidelines and allocated resources

- *Protective*—of each other against outside threats

- *Unbound*—has high aims, with the workforce on board for the journey ahead

- *Focused*—commits to completion while course-correcting or navigating around obstacles and delivers results
- *Essence*—is able to boil down early any emerging trends or problems

- *Proud*—deeply believes in "winning is everything"; team success outweighs individual glory

- *Trust-Centered*— courage to fail and learn

- *Strategically Values Information*—early adopters of technology for broad-based functional excellence

- *Talent Magnet*— home to highly diverse, world-class technical and leadership talent

(*continued*)

Relationship-Centric Best Practice:
Blue Print for High-Performing Teams (Continued)

INDIVIDUAL COMPETENCIES	TEAM DYNAMICS	RELATIONSHIP- CENTRIC ORGANIZATIONS
• *Mastery*—*is* naturally inquisitive; education is a lifelong process	• *Respect*—earned through thought leadership and consistent value-add both within and external to the team	• *Purposeful*— long-term vision consistently shared and nurtured

In the book *The War for Talent*, the authors describe a pervasive talent mindset as a deep conviction shared by leaders throughout the company that sustainable competitive advantage in the next two decades can come only from having better talent at all levels. Alarming statistics point to the undisputable fact that emerging markets such as China and India are producing more honor students than we have students, with unprecedented access to evolutionary technology at a drastically reduced acquisition cost. Although I am bullish on the United States's resiliency, I remain skeptical about our ability to win this global war. How long will it take for these countries to outpace the U.S. knowledge economy? How long before we relinquish the intellectual capital advantage?

Greg Alexander, a personal friend and CEO of Sales Benchmarking Index (SBI) recently conducted a market research in partnership with Career Point Consulting. They interviewed 25,000 sales reps asking for descriptions of their ideal job. Where Greg's previous work with Dr. Brad Smart on *Topgrading for Sales* was primarily focused on the buy-side with insights from hiring sales managers, this survey focused on the sell-side: what kind of a company did top-producing sales reps want to work for. The results were shocking, that, as attributes such as a strong compensation plan,

competitive territory, and enterprise sales volumes were expe..... ,
the resounding response could be summarized with:

*I'm looking for a company to invest in me as an individual and a
home where I can build a long-term career.*

"This clearly validates a high interest and value in relationships from the company to these high-performing sales professionals," commented Greg.

Their research also highlighted that during the decade (1996
to 2006), sales turnover was estimated to be between 38 and 42
percent in B2B sales across 19 unique industries. The replacement
costs of sales professionals, including recruiting fees, on-boarding,
training and development, salary, commission, and benefits were
estimated to be close to $500,000 per rep. With roughly 20 million
professionals in the United States alone who classify themselves in
B2B sales functions, the sales turnover translates to an estimated
eight million sales reps every year. At $500,000 each, that is a $400
billion problem in the United States every year.

Do you still believe the global war for talent is not a
costly one?

The Misperceived Value of a Rolodex

Ask any sales manager what the top qualities they want in the
next great sales hire are and I would be surprised if a strong
Rolodex wasn't near the top of that list. But if you carefully consider its characteristics, the Rolodex itself is purely transactional.
Its perceived or underlying value is desired relationships which,
by definition, lead to accelerated access, enhanced go-to-market,
or extended reach at a much more attractive cost of sales.

Unfortunately, like many transactional measures, a Rolodex
seldom has the means to represent more than its quantity. Two
greater attributes often missed in the analysis of the ultimate
value of that Rolodex are the diversity or quality of the individuals it contains. What percentage of that Rolodex includes C- or
V-level executives? How long have those relationships existed?

Could you document a natural quality progression of those relationships? How many are invested in daily? What has been the documented repeat or referral business from that Rolodex? Has the inherent built-in trust ever been battle tested?

Author of *Topgrading for Sales*, Greg Alexander, along with Dr. Brad Smart, gathered interesting insights from over 6,000 interviews with sales professionals over a 20-year period. The research highlighted that many publically traded companies demanded monthly or quarterly quota performance from their sales organizations, a practice that resulted in a strong short-sighted focus by the individual sales reps. This high transaction-centric focus versus investment in the longer-term viability of key relationships toward establishing a foundational level of trust was identified as a major mistake.

"I attribute the success of individual reps to three critical areas: 10 percent knowledge, 10 percent luck, 80 percent relationships," commented Greg. "Sales professionals with long-term careers who have succeeded through various economic cycles, selling for multitudes of companies understand and leverage the transferability of their personal brands."

Relationship Economics @ Work: Greg Alexander at SBI and Transformation Business Development

Greg Alexander called me for this interview from the Accenture Match Play Golf Tournament in beautiful Tucson, Arizona, where he had been requested to give a keynote speech on the strategic value of sales benchmarking to a group of 30 chief sales officers. This exclusive three-day event encompassed educational forums and collaborative discussions as well as a black-tie gala with significant others.

"We are a small but growing company and simply wouldn't have the resources to put on an event of this caliber together for top sales officers at marquee companies such as Sun, BMC, PepsiCo, Best Buy, and Unisys, to name a few," Greg explained. "This opportunity was only possible due to my investment and relationship with Rick Bakosh, managing partner in the Accenture CRM service line with responsibility for Accenture's Sales Transformation solutions."

Greg first met Rick a year ago and resisted the temptation to push for getting into their accounts and start comparing deal pipelines. He invested the time, effort, and resources to understand Rick's needs and contributed content, introduced him to influential relationships, and helped his staff with different challenges, none as fee work.

"When this opportunity came up, he asked if I wanted to be involved," said Greg. "Conversely, early on in launching our company, I tried to sign regional value-added sales consulting firms that were entrepreneurial with a geographic focus. Because I often went straight to conversations about deals and didn't invest in their business or our relationship, I have zero to show for that investment. I thought, acted, and treated them differently and as such, I don't have a relationship with any of them and have generated no opportunities from them since."

Greg Alexander is probably one of the sharpest sales executives I know. Yet even for seasoned sales pros, isn't it interesting that many of us often jump right into "the deal conversation" versus investing in the relationship?

Jim Collins of *Good to Great* fame is notorious for highlighting the need for asking the *who* questions and getting the right people on the bus. His research clearly outlines that people can likewise be a quantifiable strategic asset and any investment in an organization's human capital is surely to produce an above-market-rate ROI as the global war for talent continues to strengthen. Beyond the cliché that people are among an organization's greatest assets, they are also quantifiable and strategic soft assets. Similar to a brand promise, people are added to an organization because of their promise to deliver quantifiable value. Only through adherence to a systematic process of search for great talent, assessment of their appropriate fit (I'm often amazed at how many organizations "settle"); thorough on-boarding, training and development of their broad-based business acumen (versus simply their functional expertise); and consistent organizational alignment (for not only what the business needs today, but where the business is headed) and outplacement of a "wrong fit" with the least amount of disruption to the business, will an organization be able to fully gain the value of people as a strategic soft asset. That's people promise, value, and equity realized.

Strategic Relationships

Savvy HR professionals, who understand that their greatest strategic value to an organization is more than employee benefits and employee manuals, proactively invest in human capital as they aim to align culture with strategy for greater business outcomes. If you look at Figure 2.1, you'll see that as an organization searches for talent, it aims to minimize risk and maximize every individual's impact. The goal is to provide a better result through a better fit by assessing each individual's past performance as well as their unique individual characteristics. And as on-boarding continues to be improved, the hope is to also enhance individual skills and align teams for better business outcomes.

Ongoing training and development can strategically build and increase human capital value in a respective organization. But in the aim for organizational alignment, it is critical to not only grasp today's culture and strategy, but also to succinctly anticipate and define where the organization is headed in the years to come. And when the fit is simply no longer valid and some of that talent must be displaced, downsizing must be

FIGURE 2.1   Return on Human Capital.

managed to effectively reduce loss of productivity and overall morale of the organization and its presence in the market.

My question to you as a leader is this: Which part of this formula couldn't benefit from stronger relationships? Which individual contributor, team manager, or organizational leader couldn't benefit from stronger intracompany as well as externally focused relationships? From the relationships of frontline sales contributors, with their customers and distribution channels, to those of procurement professionals and their most valuable strategic suppliers—all are substantial, quantifiable, and strategic soft assets in an organization's intracompany relationships. Without them, I struggle to see how any organization, regardless of its size or industry focus, can fully maximize its operational efficiency or effectiveness (not to mention the desire to maintain and ideally gain a competitive market share).

Lack of investment in an organization's human capital and intracompany relationships goes beyond missed opportunities. At the edge of business where each individual's knowledge, talent, time, and critical relationships will translate into the organization's ability (or lack thereof) to attract top performers, repeat customers, crucial alliances, loyal suppliers, and vested shareholders, ignored investments will become cancerous to any organization. Home Depot's diminished customer-centric focus from the days of its founders, Arthur Blank and Bernie Marcus to that of Bob Nardelli, as well as the often-described dysfunctional and high command-and-control internal interactions is one such example. By swaying the culture from the original founders' values and people investments—and the relationships each Home Depot associate had developed—the "GE South" model that Nardelli and team brought turned away more engaged clients (internal and external to the organization) than it retained. Comments such as, "I can get what I need at Ace Hardware—they're friendlier" from customers or, "I'm moving on" from invaluable associates directly contributed to operating and financial metrics.

ROI Reinvented

It is critical to have a succinct understanding of not only the required business strategies today, but what the organization will demand moving forward. This includes appropriately aligning people and strategies, a candid organizational assessment, and the proactive management and agile development of an organization's relationship assets. Only then can an organization move toward improving its peak performance.

Relationship competencies—defined as skills, knowledge, and relationship-centric values—are critical for the reinvention process of ROI and encompass business strategies, an organization's culture, and its leadership requirements. They are meaningful and easily understood, addressing near- and mid-term horizons with a strong future orientation. These competencies have an impact only when fully integrated into the performance evaluation and compensation models across the entire organization—certainly not an easy feat.

Relationship-Centric Best Practice: The Process of Developing an Organization's Relationship Competencies

There are three phases to the development of an organization's relationship competencies:

The first phase is a Strategic Relationship Audit primarily focused on an organization's relationship wiring— not just *what* they do but *why*.

I have heard executives ask, "My team does not collaborate—why?" Or, "We build way too many silos—why?" Or, "Instead of success, I get overt or covert pushback for fundamental change critical to our survival success—why?" A logical, rational person would understand and embrace the changing market dynamics and respond accordingly. It's critical to understand the manner in which key intracompany interactions happen, the results from the process of engaging others, and the identification of key influencers in functional, geographic, and project-based silos.

The second phase is *Relationship DNA*, which includes drafting relationship competency models, soliciting feedback from relevant and critical stakeholders, and gaining buy-in from strategic relationships central to the business strategy execution. Drafting a top-notch team of change agents and leveraging their ability to engage and influence is the only way that any impactful change will take place.

The third phase, *Institutionalizing*, integrates key identifiers or developed competencies into appropriate management processes, consistently communicating the intentional and quantifiable value of business relationships. This is where the research of and preparation for a team or an organization's most strategic relationships comes to fruition and where you can begin to implement some of the best practices gathered across disparate parts of the organization.

Soft assets can directly contribute to the reinvention of ROI. Beyond the traditionally perceived *return on investment*, we have proven the quantifiable and strategic value of relationships in areas such as *Return on Influence, Integration, Involvement, Impact, and Image*. Let's take a closer look at each.

Return on Influence

In many pockets of our corporate hallways, conference rooms, cafeterias, project meetings, and yes, even off-site strategy sessions, informal networks can sprout in a very spontaneous, ad hoc way. Many times, logical self-interest leads individuals to collaborate (often without directive) around a common goal or shared enemy or threat. For example: research scientists working on a common disease, or investment bankers serving the same industry clients, or dissenters of a new proposed government regulation. In situations like these, individuals will openly share their time, knowledge, talent, and influential relationships.

A study of social networks clearly emphasizes an exponentially higher level of diversity and quality of sources and flow of information among these informal networks than does a hierarchical structure (see the section on Return on Integration). The ability to create value is increasingly driven by the intellectual and social styles of knowledge workers. Their ability to engage and influence others, often without the authority to do so, creates considerably further reaching and faster access to customers, invaluable industry resources, and new untapped markets. They leverage their reputation of trust, which is one of a consistent pattern of predictable behavior.

Corporate leaders who are able to identify and harness key sources of influence in these informal networks can effectively replace traditionally bureaucratic and outdated matrix structures. They can facilitate the creation and socialization of highly unique intellectual capital, as well as further develop and nurture the personal relationships among key members of the talent pool.

Long-term, mutual loyalty between an employee and employer is quickly diminishing (unlike prior generations). Only by applying the energy and influence of a highly diverse group of professionals can leaders effectively align personal interests with those of the team or the organization's future aspirations.

Relationship Economics @ Work: Mac McClelland, Super Hub

During a recent trip to Dubai, United Arab Emirates (UAE), I was introduced to Mac McClelland, a retired Marine Corps major. For the past 11 years, McClelland has been leveraging his contacts in the Middle East to help companies around the world broker deals in Iraq and beyond. For companies that don't know their way around the Middle East and want to do business there, Mac's your man. He is the classic example of a quantifiable strategic relationship.

"Most of the business we get is referred through colleagues and friends," McClelland said. "It has been very helpful to have deep-rooted, long-term, proven relationships in the Middle East from living and working out here for three decades. I have an expanding address book of contacts and resources that make it much easier for American companies to leverage my relationships into productive business than to start from scratch."

Before going into business for himself, McClelland, who speaks fluent Arabic, served as the political adviser to the admiral who runs the U.S. Navy's Central Command, which oversees naval operations in the Middle East and Central Asia. After retiring in 1996, he worked as a general manager overseeing Middle East operations for Enron. His trusted relationships with high-positioned local officials in the region have led to engagements with companies to bid on a contract to supply automobiles to the new Iraqi police force; a deal with a scrap metal company based in Houston

(*continued*)

Relationship Economics @ Work:
Mac McClelland, Super Hub (Continued)

that wants to bid on the remains of Iraqi tanks blown up by U.S. bombs; and to various consulting roles to major U.S. companies such as 3M to help them break into the Iraq market. He even helped the Saudis develop their marine corps.

In 2003, McClelland leveraged his relationships to put together a team to build a military base in the Middle East for the U.S. Air Force. By the first night, they had 500 airmen in air-conditioned tents. By the next night, they were able to provide hot and cold running water, toilets, and showers. By the third day, hot meals were on hand.

"Not only was it the weekend, but it was an Islamic holiday," McClelland said. "Had we not had the relationships in the region, this would have been an almost impossible task. As it turned out, we exceeded all expectations of the U.S. Air Force and met a service standard they never expected anyone in the region to achieve."

When asked what he thought were the top mistakes U.S. companies make in their attempts to expand in the region, number one on his list was our impatience to make the required investments of time and human capital to build and nurture relationships. Instead, he said, U.S. companies tend to parachute in without spending the time it takes to build relationships.

"Cultures in this part of the world insist on knowing you before they will do business with you," McClelland said. "The relationship is fostered through many meetings where business is not discussed. Instead, they try to gauge you as a person to see how you value family and friends and what your intentions are—both those that are visible and those you don't share. Once you have earned their trust and developed the relationship, only then will business be introduced."

Return on Integration

Corporate executives invest enormous resources in long range, yet shortsighted, strategic plans as evidenced by countless initiatives that become obsolete by the sheer dynamics of their markets and competitors. Technological advances, evolving regulations, and social dynamics also affect this obsolescence. Yet many corporate leaders ignore the strategic opportunity to create a truly sustainable competitive differentiation and one of the highest returns with a substantially lower investment of money and risk exposure: creating a highly integrated organization of decentralized relationships.

As succinctly illustrated in Rod Beckstrom's book *The Starfish and the Spider*, the massively complex and dynamic ecosystems of today's highly matrixed corporations can more effectively adapt to the market dynamics by way of decentralized competency teams. Substantial organizational inertia creates difficult personality dynamics, and also has the potential to bring out highly destructive corporate politics in any effort to drive meaningful change. Our research, coupled with the digitization of social networks, highlights a strategic asset in any manager, leader, or executive's investment of time and energy in not only creating decentralized teams, but also in nurturing productive relationships in their dynamic environments.

In contrast to the Industrial Age—in which much of the current command and control organizational structure was focused on capital as the most valuable resource—the current multigenerational workforce leverages a very different asset for creating shareholder value. The highly integrated business unit, operating company, or division, which mobilizes and leverages its broad-based intellectual capital, tends to waste fewer cycles in redundant market penetration, talent acquisition, and strategic supplier relationships. Instead, their intracompany, as well as external relationship development efforts, can translate into not only more rewarding, productive work for its current and future talent, but also a greater Return on Capital at a relatively low risk.

Return on Involvement

Many people believe that the sheer number of extra curricular activities will enhance overall market presence—particularly in professional services, where it is considerably more difficult to elevate your intangible value-add. But simply joining 15 boards and showing up for meet and greets will not suffice. A much tighter focus on a prioritized select few, with a greater impact on execution, is the answer to stronger market presence. Your involvement with any intracompany forum to exchange ideas— as well as the more traditional externally focused avenues such as industry associations, professional affiliations, or accreditation bodies—all demand a considerable investment of your limited time, effort, and resources. Although many understand intuitively the potentially influential and certainly the equity value of their involvements, very few measure the actual cost— much less the opportunity cost.

I am involved in well over a dozen organizations, such as the National Speakers Association, the Institute of Management Consultants, American Management Association, the Society of International Business Fellows, Association for Corporate Growth, and Friends of Scouting, to name a few. In the past, I used to attend their various functions, volunteer for countless causes, and became immersed in each of their respective missions. But when you continue to attend and provide ideas and insights and your time, capital, and introductions to influential relationships, when do you ever get a chance to ascertain a return on your involvement? In my case, I even reached a point of diminishing returns in which critical personal and professional relationships were being neglected at the cost of attending yet another event or function, engaging with people or organizations I didn't much care for. By reducing the sheer *quantity* and focusing on a select few most applicable to your personal and professional goals and objectives, you not only create more discretionary time – but the investments you choose to make will tend to create a higher return.

Generally, three fundamental functions become the critical arteries of an organization's sustainability: membership, programming, and fundraising. To maximize your return on involvement, take a leadership role in one of these critical functions. Join a few select boards, and through the execution of critical milestones, you'll earn the trust and respect of your peers to exert influence from that active and impactful involvement. Choose fewer organizations with high quality professional members who are decidedly relevant to your personal or professional endeavors. Aim to attend or help create content-rich events with actionable takeaways, not simply a motivational rah-rah. Recommend or help create multiple revenue streams so the organization does not rely solely on membership dues or corporate sponsorships of a single annual event. And particularly in volunteer-based organizations, become the connector, the collaborator, and the consensus builder with a track record of execution.

Relationship Economics @ Work: Steve McGaw at AT&T and Relationship-Centric Problem Solving

Almost every person's most precious commodity is time. Many business relationships begin to break down when there is a perception that one side is extracting more time than they are contributing value.

Steve McGaw, SVP, Mobility Supply Chain and Fleet Operations, for AT&T, has been with the company for 20 years. His division manages more than 1,200 full-time employees in addition to some 3,000 contractors. The company usually deals with partners they know, like, and trust, but there are times when the success of the business calls for more difficult relationships.

(continued)

Relationship Economics @ Work: Steve McGaw at AT&T and Relationship-Centric Problem Solving (Continued)

"I once had a project that we were really struggling with as a company," Steve said. "We could not reach an agreement with the data company we were working with at the time and had a number of unsolved issues. Every time we got on the phone with them, they were late. When we would finally reach an agreement, they would draw up the paperwork and it would be totally different than [sic] what we were expecting."

"It is unlike me to jump on a plane and spend time with somebody without a clear agenda and purpose, but eventually, I invited them to a golf event in their city and they agreed," he said. "We spent the weekend together and hardly talked any business. We built a relationship that weekend and two weeks later, all of our business issues had been resolved."

Return on Impact

As highlighted by Larry Bossidy in his book *Execution*, when people, processes, and tools converge with a mindset to execute, you realize *Return on Impact*. Those who can consistently deliver performance, execution, and results—despite macro- or microeconomic conditions, setbacks, roadblocks, and challenges—develop a reputation and quantifiable return on any investment made for their ability to perform. An organization's ability to candidly assess, proactively manage, and develop its high performing and high potential talent with a great sense of agility is a fundamental contributor to this Return on Impact.

High-potential individuals must be systematically measured on current performance and development paths for both breadth and depth of competencies and capabilities, as well as their true potential for not only becoming a leader but also their progress along this continuum (how they react to the good, the bad, and the ugly during this journey). So how do you proactively identify and systematically nurture the breadth and depth of relationship development knowledge, behavior, and skills in an up-and-comer? Fewer organizations, unfortunately, are willing to take risks with high potentials in critical roles—they're demanding high performers and high provens. So how do you assess a high potential's relationship-centric readiness to drive very real impact in the business? Here is a simple formula

Current State of Performance (competencies/skills) +
Developmental Plan (good and bad experiences, motivation) +
Potential (readiness traits) =
Relationship-Centric Readiness

That readiness has to then be questioned in context. Specifically, are they ready *now?* Will they be ready in one to two years with this additional development? In one to two years with a great deal of development? Or, should you "wait and see,"—which is a

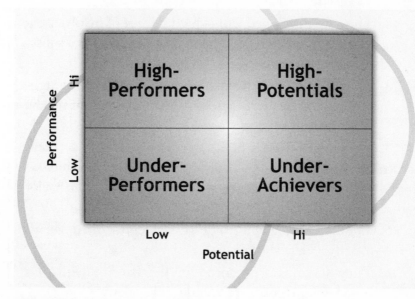

FIGURE 2.2 Return on Impact Matrix.

maintenance mode—and keep this person in her current role to see how well she adapts and respond to challenges?

The result is a return on impact matrix such as shown in Figure 2.2.

Return on Image

"When one comes across as a confident leader, a mover and shaker, they have this sense of destiny about them," commented

---

Relationship-Centric Best Practice: Personal Development Planning

A development plan requires creativity and it is incredibly difficult, if not impossible, to be creative in isolation. As such, the best development plans we've seen from our global clients have the following characteristics:

1. They are highly individualized, personalized, and localized.
2. They are developed with a high degree of involvement from both the individual participants as well as a subset of respected peers.
3. They involve a performance manager and other high-performing leaders across the organization in the development process.
4. They encompass a high degree of practical, yet new, behaviors and unique learning experiences and include a change in behavior (because only a change in behavior creates impact).
5. They employ a multitude of strategies for development.
6. They serve as a platform for the development of a broader bench of current and future talent.

Jim Boone, a friend and partner at Nosal Partner, a retained search firm. "They are straightforward in their answers, curious, bright with a lot of energy and drive." They possess what he referred as the "Wow Factor"; you get the sense that they have their act together, are going places. "I can't wait for the board to meet him."

Particularly in business relationships, the first half of the battle is looking the part. If you're interviewing for a key role—within or external to the organization and whether for a sale, to propose a project, request budgets, lead a critical initiative—and are serious about the opportunity, your part has to be complementary to the rest of the team. You have to be more right than wrong. Return on Image is less about look and much more about the confident, capable manner in which your carry yourself. That image is important and you have an opportunity to align the positive and trusted image of your organization with you as its catalyst in the circle of constituents you serve.

In a business environment that tends to err on the side of the casual versus the business, in many circles, "khakis and Polo shirts" are replacing the classic pinstriped suit. Unfortunately, many of us don't have the relationship with our peers, or fear legal retribution to comment on what is often poor judgment in our subordinate's perceived image. In a recent meeting at a law firm, I saw an otherwise seemingly competent and capable attorney sporting a black dress shirt with a black tie. When have you ever seen a professional service executive dressed in a black shirt and a tie? Last time I checked, a law firm was not an audition for *Dancing with the Stars*. Senior executives in particular take on a very different posture, demeanor, and mindset when engaging a professional, polished image. We should all feel a sense of obligation to clearly point out to the next generation of workforce that open-toed sandals, an unshaven "vacation" look, and low-cut blouses are simply inappropriate for many business environments.

I recall a very specific incident early on in my career when I wore a lower-than-acceptable-standard attire to a *Fortune* 500 employer. When my immediate manager saw my khakis, he asked if we could go downstairs to the building deli and get a cup of coffee together. He discreetly asked about my attire, and when I explained that as a co-op student, I owned only one suit and it was getting cleaned, he gave me an advance until my next paycheck to purchase a couple of dress slacks and a sport coat that day. He helped me understand that it wasn't only about the attire—it was about a professional, polished image and a demeanor worthy of confidence, respect, and trust.

Where did you learn how to dress for success? What changed in the mid- to late 1990s to suddenly shift those attributes? Many point to the current conundrum of "way too casual at times" to the Internet bubble, when skateboarding down the halls and "Beer Fridays" became trendy. But similar to the lopsidedness of the market capitalization of many of the same companies at that time, we somehow also lost sight of the value of a clean, polished professional image. I'm not advocating stiff or uncomfortable; I would simply submit that executives take a very different posture, demeanor, and mindset when engaging a professional, polished image.

This kind of image doesn't necessarily have to be expensive—simply well thought-out. Attire that is appropriately tailored for your build, colors that enhance your natural skin tone, and quality fabrics that can survive a weeklong international business trip are all examples of investments toward your Return on Image. Personally, I would always prefer to be overdressed rather than underdressed. You can always take off the tie or the jacket, but you feel—or you certainly should feel—a sense of missed opportunity or poor judgment when you are dressed inappropriately for the occasion.

Another great opportunity for more seasoned readers to mentor those who must travel for professional endeavors is to help them learn how to travel *well*. For men, this includes always bringing extra dress shirts, ties and collar stays. For professional women (compliments of my business partner Jennifer), you

---

Relationship-Centric Best Practice: Baggage Protection

Whenever possible, purchase plane tickets with your American Express card and sign up for the Premium Baggage Protection program. Under the program, if your bags are delayed, you have a spending limit to acquire what you need. If they are lost, there is extra protection to likewise purchase suits and other necessities while you are on the road.

---

should always have an extra pair of pantyhose, casual outfits for unexpected after-hour events, and clothes that don't tend to wrinkle as much. Jennifer also checks with the hotel ahead of time to see if there is a place to have clothes professionally pressed or dry-cleaned on the premises.

At a very early age, my dad drove into me the fact that polished shoes are a sign of a polished personality. I am passing that on to my young son. My mother taught me to buy fewer, but buy nicer. One of the most memorable jobs I had in my early college days was working at the famous men's clothing store, Mark Shale. As part of our training, we attended a six-week training course on how to match patterns, colors, and complementary blends. Here's another tip: learn how to tie a bowtie. My grandfather taught me how to do this in front of a mirror. They look considerably more polished than clip-ons, and they are often great conversation starters to engage others at social or professional gatherings.

Take the time to learn about patterns. When in doubt, find an image consultant or go to a fine men's clothing store and ask for help. Significant others can also serve as independent style consultants (just make sure they have good taste). Think simple elegance as many people make up their minds within seconds of approaching you to start a conversation at a personal or

Relationship-Centric Best Practice: Professional Demeanor

Another major contributor to Return on Image is a professional demeanor. This includes:

- Having the education and experience to support a strong sense of self-esteem and self-confidence, yet the humility to continue to learn and grow.
- Discretion at company-related functions.
- Paying the utmost attention to hygiene.
- A diverse and broad-based exposure to a variety of experiences.

If you are a decent golfer, can ski, have been deep sea fishing, and understand the basic tenets of polo, for example, you are much more likely to be invited to high-profile events with a far greater concentration of influential contacts.

professional gathering, and most people have a deep sense of appreciation for a professional, polished look. They want to associate with apparently other equally successful individuals in the room.

Former Federal Reserve Board chairman Alan Greenspan has always had a competent, authoritative aura about him. He may not be the ideal cover for a fashion magazine, but his image is extremely simple and sincere with a sense of seniority, respect, and trust. How is your image perceived and described to others? Is it an asset or a liability? What has to happen for you to realize the need and invest critical resources to create a quantifiable return on your image?

3

Strategic Relationship Planning

T hough most people agree that relationships are important, few actually bother to measure, quantify, or leverage them to their fullest potential. And even though every organization creates an annual sales plan – in which they craft and strategize around an annual marketing and operating plan – we've yet to find one that says, "For us to be successful in reaching these key goals and objectives, we need to identify, build, nurture, and leverage these relationships and here is how we'll get there."

As with any strategic initiative, the planning process is considerably more valuable than the actual plan itself. In this chapter, I discuss the eight-stage process that includes the templates, worksheets, and filtering mechanisms necessary to create a personal, team, and organization-wide strategic relationship plan. In the example section of a strategic relationship plan for a professional services firm, I cover topics such as:

- *Relationship-Centric Goals*—business goals that you simply cannot achieve alone and must develop and nurture critical relationships to attain
- *Relationship Bank*—existing relationships with diversity and quality of those relationships as critical as the sheer quantity
- *Pivotal Contacts*—those who have already seen the movie and have been through the pitfalls you're headed for; highly influential relationships you must seek to develop because they are instrumental to your future success
- *Relationship Currency Exchange*—the promised and delivered value in the favor economy, and
- *30-60-90–Day Personal Action Plans*—critical to relationship development and a nurturing process based on a quantifiable and prioritized set of metrics

Fundamental Flaw in Strategic Planning

In 1972, Richard Rumelt, a professor of strategy at UCLA's Anderson School of Management, became the first person to uncover a statistical link between corporate strategy and profitability. He concluded that moderately diversified companies outperformed more diversified ones—a discovery that has held up after more than 30 years of research. His controversial 1991 paper *How much does industry matter?*, published in the *Strategic Management Journal*, highlights that neither industry nor corporate ownership can explain the lion's share of differences in profitability among business units. In short, he reinforced the notion that being good at what you do matters a lot more than what industry you are in.

This is in stark contrast to the 1980s, when the conventional wisdom dictated that an organization generates strategic plans at a business unit level and subsequently rolls up those plans in a portfolio fashion for the senior management of the company. In recent years, much of the strategy work has once again become recentralized. According to Rumelt, most corporate strategic plans have little to do with strategy. Instead, they are simply three-to-five-year rolling resource budgets and best guestimates of market share projections, and they often create a false expectation that this exercise will produce a coherent strategy.

Strategic plans must outline a succinct pathway to substantially higher performance, making the need for strategic planning more event-based and mandated by the dynamic changes in one's industry. Planning should be based on available resources instead of becoming simply an annual exercise. Most companies link their strategy execution to that formulation by exploiting changes in the environment such as technology, customer preference, regulations, cost of required resources, or competitive landscape.

If your strategy begins with identifying changes in your environment, then certainly reviewing changes in your current and available talent, the enhanced or diluted value of your brands, and the diversity and quality of your critical relation-ships—in essence, your soft assets—must also be included in developing strategies for exploiting those changes. Some may have long-term consequences, such as a brain drain with retiring, mature, and Baby Boomer generations. Companies must take a position now and invest in critical resources and processes to capture and capitalize on their soft assets before they are lost.

Strategic relationship thinking helps us take a consistent position in an uncertain world. Uncertainty and ambiguity will always be omnipresent. In many ways, they are the flip side of opportunity. If you are uncomfortable with uncertainty, you can always wait for others to take a first mover position and ascertain their critical success factors. Although this does minimize risk, you will also lose the opportunity to take advantage of that knowledge at the edge.

Another fundamental challenge with strategic planning is that, in many circles, it is shortsighted. It is difficult to see a quantifiable ROI on your brand, for example, in one quarter. Typical budgeting processes start with a mission statement that outlines an often vague aim or goal of the business, followed by a typical offsite strategic planning session to set the direction and high-level goals of the entire organization. These often form the framework for a six-month investment of critical resources such as human capital and time, not to mention 30 percent-plus of a senior executive's and financial manager's bandwidth.

The struggling Ford Motor Company recently discovered that this process can be a $1.2 billion drain. According to Jeremy Hope and Robin Fraser's book, *Beyond Budgeting*, a decade-old benchmarking study highlighted that the average company invests more than 25,000 *person days* per $1 billion of revenue in planning a performance management process. The often more intellectually engaging and analytically trackable issue of strategy can become an obsession for managerial attention because it is simply sexier to talk about strategy, even though a great deal of strategy literature highlights that focus and time are scarce resources.

It's critical to recognize the common temptation to attempt to fix what doesn't need fixing or to grossly ignore a critical component of the planning process. The common misconception that soft assets—similar to soft skills—cannot be quantified and as such cannot be planned for can deter even a well thought-out plan. Or, worse yet, people abdicate to HR or Learning and Development, but only in strict alignment with the current and anticipated requirements of the business.

Strategic Relationship Planning

Strategic Relationship Planning (SRP) is the process of transforming an organization's most valuable relationships into quantifiable performance, execution, and results. It is designed to help you identify fundamental key market opportunities and the resources you will need to meet these goals, including past strategic relationships and those necessary to achieve success moving forward. The plan enables an individual to achieve business goals and objectives and should be tightly aligned with those of the organization. Contrary to many plans disguised as management oversights, strategic relationship plans are driven by the efforts, analysis, and insights from individual relationship investments. What did you learn from those investments? Would you make them again if given the opportunity?

If you believe that past results are indicative of future performance, you must begin with a historical perspective of your past results to strategically outline the relationships most valuable to your individual team or organizational efforts.

Eight Pillars of Strategic Relationship Planning

Eight fundamental areas where strategic relationships can and should be most impactful make up the pillars of a Strategic Relationship Plan. These pillars dictate where to compete, how to compete, and the quantifiable value of the strategic relationships you desire.

Pillar 1: Strategic Focus

What business are you in? What business *should* you be in? Although simple in their inquisitive nature, it is amazing just how complex these two questions can be.

What business you are in should answer, from a historical perspective, where you have been most successful, where you have produced the most professional products and services, and where your team's core competencies and expertise lie. Beyond those internal factors, the business you are in considers what the market has paid for and the value you have brought to the table.

What business you *should* be in is really what Dr. Roch Parayre at Mack Center for Technological Innovation at Wharton School of Business calls "scanning the periphery." By changing the tools and focus from certainty to risk, and from ambiguity to chaos, you elevate your perspective from lower risk and lower reward to higher risk and higher reward.

Relationships Economics @ Work: Dr. Roch Parayre and Scenario Planning

The genesis of the scenario planning methodology, Parayre explains, originated with the oil industry. Big oil companies who relied on oil from the turbulent Middle East had to plan for different scenarios that could affect their business, such as war or embargo.

"We live in a world that is increasingly uncertain, yet most organizations plan as if the world were predictable," said Parayre. "We make forecasts. We plan for one view of the future. But when that view ends up not playing out as we'd

(continued)

Relationships Economics @ Work:
Dr. Roch Parayre and Scenario Planning (Continued)

planned, we are ill prepared for the alternative. Scenario planning not only reduces risk, it provides a much broader perspective on both opportunities and threats in your strategy."

Today, Parayre and his partners at Decision Strategies International, Inc. work with companies primarily in the financial services, pharmaceutical, and IT industries—all industries that twist in the wind of some major regulatory uncertainties.

Scenario planning forces these companies to ask themselves if their current strategy is *future proofed* across different scenarios. Relationships play an important role in this process because, for each initiative, specific relationships needed for each possible outcome must be identified and nurtured.

For example, if you're a pharmaceutical company, the idea of a "Hillary-type" health care system is clearly an issue.

"If you are a health care player anywhere in the health care value chain, you might have relationships with the kind of free marketers who serve you well in our current system," Parayre said. "But because this value chain can change, you must also begin developing relationships with some of the government entities you might have shied away from in the past. If a single payer entity emerges, you will need to be able to leverage regional relationships in every possible way. If you have only built relationships that you need based on one set of assumptions about the future, you may be in bad shape if the future plays out in a different way."

"The relationship story is very consistent with the option story. The more options you have at the periphery of your core, the more you are prepared for multiple futures," Parayre said. "The same story applies to relationships. The more relationships you have as options, the more prepared you will be to leverage those relationships and deepen them if a particular future plays out."

As I cover in Pillar 7—Competitive Differentiation—later in this section, you must scan both internal and external influences in the short and long term, and focus narrowly on your products and services and the broader market category in which you play. But beyond the competitive and market intelligence often encapsulated in a typical strategic focus, in Strategic Relationship Planning, you must also include business intelligence, environmental scanning, and, to some level, social intelligence, the correlation between behaviors and relationships, as described in the book *Social Intelligence: The New Science of Success* by Karl Albrecht.

Said another way, the business you should be in is all about asking credible and trusted sources of strategic relationships the right questions. These sources could include current and prospective customers in an advisory board role, industry or functional insiders, and often ignored or underdeveloped cross-industry insights. You must learn from past interactions—what are your blind spots (what is happening now, best practices from other industries, and so forth) and who in your industry has a knack for identifying weak signals and early trends and acting on them ahead of the competition?

You must also examine present relationships—what important factors are you rationalizing away? What are perceived industry thought leaders and Mavericks saying and doing? What are your customers and strategic suppliers really thinking? How can you get to them at a deeper, more candid level regarding what is happening right now?

Third, you have to anticipate surprises that can hurt you and conversely, uncover what can really help you. Are there some emerging technologies that can help you change the game? Remember that there is a slight difference between incrementalism and innovation. Innovation is doing it *differently*. Incrementalism is doing it *better*. Some label incrementalism as continuous improvement and in many instances that works fine. Is there a model way of doing something that you haven't explored because of whatever constraints you are under now? Competitive advantage is a highly fluid moving target and a consistent review of your critical assumptions about your fundamental strategic focus is critical to long-term success. Strategic relationships can provide the much needed independent perspective and perhaps unique insights on one's strategic focus.

Pillar 2: Revenue Growth

I continue to be baffled by the lessons we didn't learn from the technology bubble bursting in 2001. I don't care what business you are in, you cannot buy something for $2, sell it for $1, and make it up in volume!

How efficient is your sales, marketing, and business development efforts? How effective are they? Beyond 10 pounds of PowerPoint at the next leadership meeting, how do you know? Profitable revenue growth is about systematic, disciplined, strategic named or global account planning processes. Specifically, it is how to identify, nurture, and leverage your most valuable relationships for the specific intent of driving revenue at the most attractive cost of that revenue acquisition. How do you accelerate your organization's profitable revenue growth?

Pillar 3: Cost Performance

A very strong trend in the market today is that of supplier relationship management. Simply put, it delineates your broad-based list of suppliers in a pyramid-like format with the tactical, commodity-centric ones (you can get copper wiring from 50 different vendors tomorrow) all the way up to truly strategic, long-term suppliers instrumental to your success in the market (Motorola handsets for AT&T Mobility, for example).

Think of the different levels in this pyramid. Commodities are just that—commodity suppliers are all put through reverse auctions and will aim to drive a more attractive cost structure and leverage information technology to constantly scan the market for value chain disruption.

Relationship-Centric Best Practices:
Strategic Supplier Relationship Management

Telecommunications giant AT&T purchases devices from six primary providers. It also uses a small network of data providers, with which it collaborates to develop next-generation technology.

Some devices, such as handsets, are purchased on an ongoing RFP basis, which is a very rigorous structured process with many geographic restrictions. However, there are other, more strategic services that the company partners with to provide its customers.

"Our relationships with our vendors are, to some degree, on a year-to-year basis," said Steve McGaw, SVP, Mobility Supply Chain and Fleet Operations for AT&T. "But with many, we have built trust with them over the years. We know that they have successfully delivered on smaller projects, so we are more likely to collaborate with them on larger projects in the future."

The best and most recent example of this, McGaw said, is the Apple iPhone. "Steve Jobs had a concept (and so did we) that they could create a unique Apple phone with a unique Apple experience," he said. "One of the services we wanted to offer was that of visual voicemail, where your phone shows you who left a voicemail message and when they left it. Then, the user can select which one he wants to listen to without having to dial in and listen to them all sequentially. Our relationship with Apple drove our two companies to develop the technology together so that it could be delivered on the first iPhone."

(continued)

Relationship-Centric Best Practices:
Strategic Supplier Relationship Management (Continued)

"In this situation," McGaw said, "we had to adapt and leverage relationships on multiple levels to ultimately deliver a new service offering. Visual voicemail was something we were innovating ourselves here at A&T and making progress on it, but the catalyst of the iPhones and Apple's commitment to launch the product—and the relationships at multiple levels within the two companies—is what ultimately drove it to success."

Conversely, you have foresight into strategic suppliers' advanced research and development efforts because they are an extension of your own research and development efforts. Collaboration often drives unique products and services to a very differentiated and sustainable market position. Cost performance in Strategic Relationship Planning also points to unparalleled asset management efficiency and effectiveness through critical relationships. If I am Sara Lee, for example, and have an on-site account team at the Wal-Mart headquarters in Bentonville, Arkansas, I am not only tightly integrated with Wal-Mart buyers, but can also optimize my asset utilization much more efficiently and effectively and exponentially increase my inventory turnover ratios.

Pillar 4: Process Optimization

There is a reason that a number of franchise concepts succeed. They follow a systematic, disciplined process for success. How do you build repeatable, predictable processes to scale your business? The answer is through strategic relationships.

World-class project and process management is independent of any one person, entity, or potential constraint. It is, however, highly driven by collaboration in constantly looking at what is working, why, and how it can be continually optimized to get the best outcome. That collaboration comes from internal pockets and external constituents with a vested interest in the outcome of that process. It is critical here to identify key touch points, milestones, and required resources along that process continuum. Then, look for quality gates of governance and compliance to best practices for the most efficient flow.

Pillar 5: Talent Development

As we have said before, your human capital is your greatest asset. The question is how to find, attract, and retain top talent and effectively invest in your employees to realize the greatest ROI on your human capital.

Did you know that many of your current employees come with built-in relationships? You can exponentially enhance your talent acquisition efforts by focusing on the top-notch talent that you already have. There is a likely chance that your best employees know other highly qualified, capable talent, for whom you are currently searching across the hall or across the globe.

Performance evaluation has to be one of the most dreaded events by both managers and employees alike. Givers don't want to do them—and neither do takers. They tend to all pile up in the last hour of the month, quarter, or year before HR calls and complains—and then they typically go something like this: How are you? Things are fine. How are the kids? Life is good. You suck and that's it. And unless you force the conversation back to the "you suck" part, these evaluations don't really become effective.

This is not the time to argue or declare, "Everyone hates me" and just move on. What we're talking about is *candor* and it's the much needed, less politically correct, much more productive way to retain and develop talent. After all, you can't do anything about a reputation you don't know.

"People gravitate toward those who create influence—people who are most self-aware. This includes asking tough questions such as 'What I am good at, not good at, am passionate about doing, what am I really about, what do I believe strongly in'; people who are self-aware are at the highest levels of accomplishment" comments Dan Brown, a friend and former SunTrust executive.

"Instead of performance reviews—a bunch of paperwork—I like 360-degree assessments. What do people around you think of you, what do people above you think of you—give the person a sense of their perceived value-add; usually, here are your strengths and weaknesses, what to work on, and what doesn't work. People will tell you about your blind spots much more so than the core evaluation" he added.

Bob Danzig, former head of the Hearst Newspaper Group and vice president of the Hearst Corporation, recently described what he calls the cream of the crop in every organization—*destiny shapers and future builders*. Only through strategic relationships and a systematic plan to identify and truly seek out the DNA of the future shapers of your team and organization will you survive, much less succeed. There is a tendency for people to go into a corner and simply do it themselves. Instead, you must use internal and external relationships to identify the most critical touch points of relationships and what you should do at each of these points.

Pillar 6: Matrix Effectiveness

Organizations are complicated structures. With multiple reporting structures in different geographic locations and with different agendas, how do you get everyone on the same page to focus on execution? And more important, do you know *how* things really get done?

We believe that a highly decentralized and often informal network of relationships contributes more to actual productivity than the traditional organizational chart. Take a look at Figure 3.1. On the left is a very traditional organizational chart—many readers of this book are in one. It is hierarchical in nature and represents the classic command and control model originally conceived in

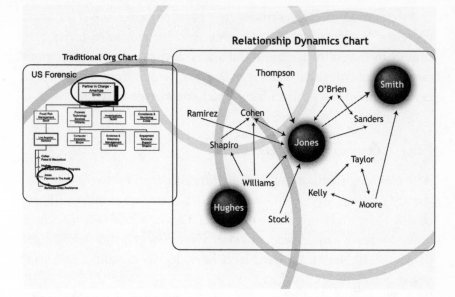

FIGURE 3.1   Relationship Dynamics Chart and Traditional Org Chart.

military circles since before World War I. Conversely, the Relationship Dynamics Chart maps sources of information flow as indicated by the arrows highlighting centers of influence, sources of impact, and the true nature of collaboration at work. Someone once called this process, *mapping the water cooler.*

At the center of the Relationship Dynamics Chart is Jones. Jones has been with the organization for 10 years. She knows everyone, their spouses, their children, where they vacation, and their biggest assets and challenges both at and away from work. Conversely, Smith, as the leader of this team, has become so bogged down with administrative functions that he has actually become a bottleneck and an inhibitor to getting things done. In many ways, his finger is no longer on the pulse of the business.

Hughes is brilliant, but a raving introvert and a low talker. Because his ideas are seldom solicited or heard, his brilliance often slips under the radar and his insights are left undetected. As a result, he has become a highly underused resource when dealing with key performance indicators, balance scorecards, and matrix forecasting.

Knowledge management is not a system—it's a process. Only by sharing the current highly influential role of Jones with others in diversified functional roles and geographic locations can you decentralize and capitalize on Jones's influence, as well as potential opportunities for shared knowledge and insights.

Pillar 7: Competitive Differentiation

The challenge with competitive differentiation is that it is a constantly moving target—it's never holistic and often not evidence-based. How do you really know what a competitor is up to? Sure, you can read white papers and analyst reports, but seldom are these insights based on hard facts provided by customers or users of the competitor's products.

The other challenge with most competitive insights is that you are often looking in the rearview mirror. It is very difficult to make real-time decisions, if not forward-looking ones, based not only on competitors' products and service offerings today but on some anticipations or predictions of the direction in which they are headed. Keep in mind—it is less expensive to innovate than to advertise.

Another insight someone gave me years ago – which I regret not following more proactively – is that your market is insightful and brilliant. Find, create and invent ways to shorten the time from information to insight, insight to knowledge, and knowledge into results and performance between your market and your response to it. There is no faster path to success than through strategic relationships with market makers who have the ability to facilitate that accelerated access.

Pillar 8: Corporate Reputation

The fundamental drivers of corporate reputation begin with industry image. Regardless of how strong a company you may be, some industries—pornography, alcohol, and even tobacco, to a lesser extent—will always have a negative connotation associated with them.

But outside of this, there are some very critical components of corporate image and identity that contribute to your reputation. They include character, culture, competitiveness, the respective abilities of the CEO and employees, resources leveraged by the company, the quality, value, and range of products and services, the behavior of the leadership, and the company's profit aims and various stakeholder values. Corporate reputations, as a result of all of these things, tend to become one of esteem, trust, respect, and confidence and are inherently either good or bad. (See Figure 3.2.)

Whereas the components of the corporate image and identity are perceptual, a company's reputation is often emotional and the outcome a *superbelief*. Though no one company is always good or always bad, soley by reputation we make decisions to buy their stock, buy their products and services, work for them, or refer our friends and families—based purely on

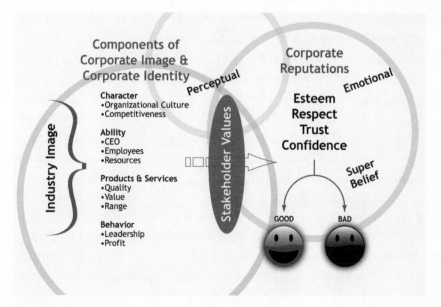

FIGURE 3.2   Critical Attributes of Corporate Reputation.

their reputation. And while corporate reputation can take years to build, it can take just an instant to destroy.

Strategic Relationship Plan for a Professional Service Firm

What follows is an outline for an annualized strategic relationship plan for partners of a professional services firm. Such a plan should be reviewed monthly for achievement of execution milestones and quarterly for strategic viability. You should also identify an accountable peer and proactively communicate with her about your progress. Develop a personal board of advisers to serve as a sort of air traffic control for some of the more challenging strategic relationship discussions.

Section 1: Looking Back—A Historical Perspective

Begin with a historical perspective of the previous year's marketing and business development efforts. Review what we refer to as your relationship-centric goals, which are business goals and objectives that mandate strategic relationships to achieve. Also include the specific relationship development efforts you made to not only achieve each goal, but your overall results for the previous year. Emphasize the *who* success stories here and ask the *who* questions I discussed earlier. This does not mean highlighting what you did to succeed, but instead which relationships most appropriately enabled you to achieve significant milestones and your overall success.

Next, quantify the outcomes of your collaboration efforts during the previous year. Keep the focus client-centric by naming the client-specific colleagues and other consultants you introduced and the results you accomplished through collaboration.

- What did you do last year to collaborate with a purpose and what were the results of that collaboration? (Most people have a lot of meetings for the sake of having meetings without solving client-centric problems.)

- Describe additional relationship-centric accomplishments made during the previous year.

Section 2: Looking Forward

The real aim of Strategic Relationship Planning is forward-looking and future proofing. Invest the time and effort to consider the following objectives.

Your Current Relationship Bank

Set aside most individuals' desires to meet new people. Many do a terrible job getting their arms around the relationships they already have. Beyond the perception that it's all about quantity, they neglect to understand and truly leverage the diversity and *quality* of their relationships. They don't realize that the more diverse the sources of interesting and relevant contacts, the broader your sphere of influence. Likewise, the higher the business stature of one's diverse Relationship Bank members, the more likely access to and opportunities with influential relationships he seeks.

But you can't possibly improve anything you don't measure, so start with the fundamentals regarding the clarity, accuracy, and relevancy of your current portfolio of relationships by asking the following questions:

- How current is the information in your personal contact list? Are contacts appropriately categorized to reflect the diversity and quality of those relationships?
- Besides basic contact information, what initial insights have you captured regarding the nature of the relationship? What are your current plans to enhance the information you track on your most valuable relationships?

- How often did you review your entire portfolio of relationships in an effort to enhance that portfolio?
- How succinctly have you identified your ideal relationship profile, including key characteristics critical for lasting and consistent year-after-year personal and professional growth through those relationships as compared to short-term transactions?
- How aligned is your list of target relationships for the upcoming year with that ideal relationship profile?
- Did you neglect some key relationships in the past year? If so, what are your plans and time frames to reinvigorate them?

Your Most Valuable Relationships

You simply don't have the bandwidth to invest in everyone equally, so how do you prioritize which relationships you'll invest in? On any given day you can contact 50 people—but which 50? How are you balancing internal versus external relationships? In our experience, if it's dysfunctional within the organization, external contacts will surely see what is clearly broken.

- Who are currently your top three clients—inside or outside the organization?

Relationship-Centric Best Practice: Relationship Resource Allocation

Reappropriate limited resources to the development and nurturing of your most valuable relationships and deprioritize those relationships that are simply not providing an appropriate return on your relationship investments.

- How intimately do you understand their business, market, and foreseeable challenges and opportunities?
- Which industry publications do you read? Which thought leaders or analysts do you know with whom you can collaborate and anticipate some of the key challenges and opportunities?
- What are your plans to increase your knowledge base of this client's business? How well do you know the internal and external sources of knowledge, insights, and influence in their business or particular requirements?
- How did you invest in nurturing the relationship at multiple business stature levels this past year? Fundamentally, it's a risk to put all of your eggs in one basket when it comes to relationships at a single point of failure. If you only have one contact in that client department or organization, what happens if that person leaves? Will you be forced to go back and start all over again?
- How would you rate the diversity of the business relationships between the two firms?
- What are your account protection and relationship development plans for the coming year? Others are surely competing for the perceived value that you provide—do you know who they are and your unique position? How can you continue to build a barrier to entry by others? In what specific manner can you continue to bring innovative ideas and products to minimize their needs or wants to explore other options or relationships?
- Has this client referred you to other relationships? Do you know why or why not?
- Are the results from your relationships with this client producing a positive trend in your business as evidenced by increased profitability from work with this client? If it's an internal relationship, is the quality of your interactions increasing? Are you being perceived or described as the go-to person? Why and how or why not?

- Asked independently, how would this client describe your relationship as well as overall reputation?
- How battle tested is your relationship with this client? Remember, relationships and trust in particular can take years to develop and only single incidences to dilute or destroy. How solid is your levy against rising waters of missed commitments and could it survive a Katrina-sized incident of poor contingency planning, lack of communication, the blame game, and a disaster of unparalleled financial or reputational outcomes?

Relationship Currency Exchange

With every interaction, we all promise value. As that value is delivered, you begin to exchange *Relationship Currency*. It's very similar to cash in its liquidity but it also has a shelf life. People may or may not remember what you did for them 6, 12, or 18 months ago, but they are likely to remember the asset you were a week ago. So the timely nature of your relationship currency exchanges is critical. Therefore, ask:

- Who are your top referral sources? How do you proactively add value to each interaction? Why would they introduce you to their most trusted relationships?
- How do you thank these sources for their referrals?
- What quantifiable business have you been able to send to each of them? What efforts will you make next year to increase referrals you make to others?

Your System for Following Through

- What is your system for proactively following through with key relationships and the ones you develop? Follow up is a transaction; follow-through is a process to ensure that value *promised* is in fact, value *delivered*.

- Describe your plan in the coming year for how you will prioritize your relationship pursuits and the criteria for which you will make key investments. How often will you work on this process and how will you enhance it?
- Describe your plan for establishing a reputation for content. How will you become a thought leader in your chosen field?

Section 3: Return on Involvement

- With what organizations are you proactively involved and why? Describe your level of involvement in the past year and plans for expansion or deletion (there is no middle road) of your contribution to that particular organization.
- What quantifiable impact did you create from that involvement? Did the relationships you developed through that involvement result in any business or potential referral sources? What efforts did you make to refer business to individuals in those organizations? Elaborate why or why not.
- To what extent did you expand your intrafirm involvements with that organization?
- To what extent did you coach and mentor associates in relationship development activities? How did you help associates learn how to more effectively relate to client challenges and opportunities and enhance their return on that involvement through your influence?
- Describe your plans for the coming year to assist associates with their relationship development efforts and help them obtain valuable experiences in key interactions throughout the year. List specific associates you plan to include in client and referral source meetings and events.

Reputation Capital

- To what extent was the value you delivered to clients and referral sources recognized for its eventual impact as having been delivered by you? What was the return on objective?

- Describe specific actions you took to enhance your personal, as well as your team's and organization's intellectual capital.
- Describe speaking, writing, or industry involvements that directly contributed to your thought leadership position. How were you a servant leader in a charity or a community?

Pivotal Contacts

As previously mentioned, and something I discuss more of in upcoming chapters, Pivotal Contacts are the relationships you aspire to have. They are often individuals who are two business statures above your current perceived reach. Their time and access to influential relationships are well protected. In our experience, they are passionate about execution and pride themselves in their subject or domain expertise.

- Describe the three most effective approaches you have identified in expanding your portfolio of relationships.
- Identify the most valuable and most diverse relationship asset you gained in the past year. What are your plans to enhance these in the coming year?
- How would you describe your relationship liabilities in the past year? What will you do to mitigate similar risks in the coming year?
- How will your efforts affect the desired outcome for a key relationship you value most?
- How did you share firmwide intellectual capital with clients and referral sources?
- Describe the marketing campaigns you designed, developed and deployed to create air cover for your relationship-centric efforts.
- What specific assets (time, capital, and human) did you invest in your overall relationship development efforts in

the past year and what investments do you anticipate for the coming year?

Relationship Signature Index

Twenty unique attributes define the personal imprint that we as individuals, teams, or organizations bring to every relationship. They are often behavioral in our approach to prioritizing and investing in our most valuable relationships; collaboration with others in search of desired solutions or outcomes; relationship-centric risk identification and mitigation; our perceived versus actual reputation among our intracompany peers; and key influencers external to the organization.

- What are your relationship strengths? In which areas would you like to improve?
- Compared to your peers of equal or greater business stature within the firm, how would you rate your *Reputation Capital?*
- How important are strategic relationships to you and why?
- What initial resources can the firm provide to help you achieve your relationship-centric goals?
- What are your quantifiable 30-60-90-day milestones?

I'm often reminded of Winston Churchill's remarks that the planning process itself is as critical as the final plan produced. If you went through this high-level overview, what did you discover about the investments you're making (or are not making) in identifying, building, nurturing, and leveraging critical relationships to your success? Only by clearly understanding:

- What business outcome are you trying to achieve
- What performance you need to enhance to achieve those outcomes, and

- What skills, experiences, and behaviors you need to enhance that performance

Will any of this effort produce the ultimate results that you're seeking? In the next chapter, you'll look at the science of relationships, which may help explain why we tend to gravitate and collaborate with some colleagues more than others.

4

Understanding the Science of Social Network Analysis (SNA)

R elationship Economics is about understanding both the art *and* science of business relationships. It has been our experience that though many get the art—30-second introductions, remembering names, building rapport—few truly understand the science. The concept of Social Network Analysis (SNA) has been in existence since the 1930s and is the intersection of psychology, anthropology, sociology, organizational design and mathematics—specifically, graph theory. Its roots are ingrained in academic circles and are too complex for many to comprehend, much less apply to teams within corporations.

Many experts have attempted to bridge the gap in an effort to explain these concepts in everyday terms. For example, in his popular book, *The Tipping Point*, Malcolm Gladwell highlights the critical importance of social networks to the general public. Through illustrative stories, Gladwell uses examples of how social networks create an enormous amount of influence and acceptance of ideas and trends. (Gladwell describes Paul Revere, for example, as one of history's great "connectors" because of his relationship with various revolutionary leaders along his route and his acute understanding of the British situation.)

In this chapter, I translate SNA into practical, proven best practices in five functional areas where Relationship Economics is most applicable.

Brief Overview of Social Network Analysis (SNA)

Social Network Analysis, in its simplest term, is the process of mapping and measuring relationships and flow between people, groups, organizations, and other information/knowledge-processing entities. SNA provides both a visual and a mathematical analysis of human relationships. The term has been used as a metaphor for over a century to convey complex sets of relationships between members of a social system. In 1954, a social scientist, Jay Barnes, began using this term to denote patterns inside and outside founded groups such as tribes or families and social categories such as gender or ethnicity. In recent years, SNA has evolved from suggestive metaphors to a true analytical model in various methods and research circles.

Analysts are able to deduct key insights from a deep dive of "whole to parts" from structures to individual interactions and from behaviors to attitude. By studying the whole network, which contains specific ties or relationships between individuals, key assumptions can be made as to the frequency, quality, and expansive nature of an interaction between two individuals.

Think about it: Why do you socialize with some co-workers more than others? Why do some colleagues' names appear more often in your Sent e-mail folder than others? Give me a copy of a person's checkbook and calendar and I can tell you the breadth and depth of their relationships. The same could be said for several key attributes of individuals with whom you tend to engage considerably more often than others. A number of those attributes could be easily explained by your role or realm of responsibilities.

Tom Robey, a friend of mine and SVP of investor relations at Time Warner Cable, recently attended a relationship economics training course. It quickly became evident that his role specifically mandates the need to engage a multitude of relationships both inside and outside the organization. Likewise, Tom Varney, VP of communications at Siemens Energy and Automation, proactively engages a multitude of business unit, division, and operations leaders to drive a consistent, cohesive communication strategy. Both of their respective roles— investor relations and communications—are examples of roles that require a proactive and consistent investment in a broad base of relationships.

Other attributes of our most valued links simply include people who *get* us. These are the people who are a lot like we are and with whom we have chemistry. If you have been through any of the behavioral or psychological assessment tools such as Meyers Briggs, HBDI, or DiSC, you realize that similar profiles naturally gravitate toward each other. In short, ENTPs (extrovert, intuition, thinking, perceiving) like hanging out with other ENTPs.

The shape of a social network—whether small or more expansive, both internal and external—can also highlight the true collaborative nature of an individual or team. In other words, a group of individuals who only communicate and collaborate with one another already share the same knowledge, and to a greater extent, the same set of contacts. Conversely, a group of individuals with connections to a broader, more diverse array of social worlds is more likely to have access to a broader knowledge base and, by deductive reasoning, access to greater opportunities to overcome obstacles.

This is why it is critical to prioritize diversity as the single biggest asset in your portfolio of relationships. The broader your social network, the bigger your relationship bank and sphere of influence.

Phil Ostwalt, a national partner of the forensic practice of KPMG LLP, is one of those rare individuals who genuinely believes in relationships. And in some ways, his extensive social network is a strong asset to his professional success. Both within the firm and outside it, Phil is well known, respected, trusted, and consistently seen as not only a viable source of knowledge, but someone with access to others who can provide a very real and quantifiable value-add based on their breadth and depth of knowledge. By collaborating beyond geographic and functional limitations—a key success attribute of social networks—Phil and his colleagues developed a poignant white paper entitled "Cross-Border Investigations." It integrated global best practices introduced as a key component to good corporate governance by Adam Bates, global chairman of KPMG Forensic. The end result of their global collaboration is a highly relevant, timely, and strong illustration of the vast and decentralized expertise within the organization. This is an example of an ideal outcome of the productivity gains delivered by effective social networks.

The next most valuable asset is the *quality* of your social network. This not only represents a strong connection between individuals, but also through sheer time and a broad base of experiences, a wider pipe for information, knowledge, talent, key insights, and access to influential individuals (see Chapter 8 on Relationship Currency Deposits). As two people connect over time, the pipeline between their networks broadens and creates bigger opportunities for them to interact more often and introduce each other to additional contacts. The more Relationship Currency that is contributed to the pipeline, the bigger the network becomes.

Think about individuals you have known and worked closely with over the years, perhaps in various jobs, markets, and business statures. Would you agree that the quality of your relationship with those individuals has strengthened because of frequent interactions and exchanges of value-based information? You tend to develop a stronger bond with those who have referred to you consistently profitable business over the years. You feel genuinely closer to those on whom you have counted for an independent perspective or unique insight. In essence, the depth of those relationships and their relevancy toward your specific goals and objectives nurture certain predictability in what you say and do on a consistent basis over a period of time. We define this as *mutual trust*.

Connections within social networks are also critical for those individuals who exercise influence or act as knowledge or relationship brokers within their own social networks—as well as between diverse networks—fill structural holes. Have you ever heard someone say, "John is a go-to person. He may not have the answer, but he certainly knows someone who does." Or, "Sandy is an amazing connector. Not only does she know everyone, but she takes pride in connecting the people she knows with value-add."

Relationship Economics @ Work:
Rob Cross and Rod Beckstrom

One of the leading authorities in the area of SNA applications is associate professor Rob Cross at the University of Virginia's McIntire School of Commerce. In 2004, along with Andrew Parker—a research consultant with IBM's Knowledge and Organizational Performance Forum—Cross extensively elaborated on the role of social networks in getting things done within any organization in their book, *The Hidden Power of Social Networks: Understanding How Work Really Gets Done in Organizations*. This idea was reinforced in Ori Brafman and Rod Beckstrom's book, *The Starfish and the Spider: The Unstoppable Power of Leaderless Organizations*. Both books compare and contrast the traditional organizational chart and what we refer to as a *relationship dynamics chart*, as shown in Figure 4.1.

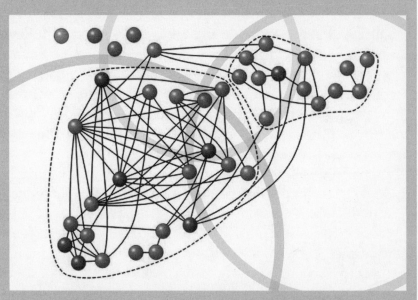

FIGURE 4.1 Multifaceted Social Network.

(*continued*)

Relationship Economics @ Work:
Rob Cross and Rod Beckstrom (Continued)

As readers of this book can appreciate, an organizational chart helps control chaos. Yet very few people believe that this is how things really get done. The hierarchical nature of an organizational chart, by sheer design, builds geographic, divisional, and functional silos that simply are not conducive to collaboration, communication, or identification and implementation of best practices across the organization.

Beckstrom masterfully compares the starfish—a highly decentralized organism—to a highly centralized command and control model of a spider. Cut off the spider's leg and you'll have a crippled spider. Cut off its head and you have a dead spider. Conversely, cut off one of the five legs of a starfish and it is likely to regenerate. Cut off all five and, in some species, you will produce five different starfish.

Have you ever wondered why it is so challenging for a true superpower such as the United States military to find one man and his group of hoodlums hiding in caves on the other side of the world? It is a classic case of a highly centralized command-and-control model trying to adapt to a much more nimble, highly decentralized cell. War, Beckstrom explains, has to become more than just a military campaign. It must also become an economic and political campaign as well.

Beckstrom highlights three ways to defeat a decentralized organization:

1. Draw them into discussion. (Blame, antagonism, and taking a hard stance seldom works.)
2. Centralize the opponent.
3. Decentralize yourself.

Characteristics of a highly decentralized model are its source of energy, driven by catalysts, ideology-centric circles or pockets of influence, and a very specific set of protocols and rules for membership that include breadth, frequency of circles, the extent of the network, funding of the network, and self-governance.

The social networking diagram highlights not only sources of influence, but the flow of information, the frequency of exchanges, and disconnected executives on the periphery—often due to the administrative nature of their roles and grossly underused resources disconnected from much of the interaction.

Organizational Application of SNA and Resulting Impact

So how does the concept of SNA apply to organizational efficiency and effectiveness? As illustrated in the relationship dynamics chart shown in Figure 4.1, social networks within organizations are defined by the organization's strategy, infrastructure, and key initiatives at any particular time.

Social networks are also often in direct conflict with managerial behaviors and organizational design. It has been our experience that performance evaluations and compensation or other incentives—as well as predetermined management practices—usually diverge from or preclude collaboration between departments, divisions, or parts of the business. As illustrated in the relationship dynamics chart, Jones, at the center of the diagram, is often and rather excessively sought out, making her a potential bottleneck.

Do you remember playing the gossip game in elementary school? The first person whispers a phrase in the ear of his neighbor and so on around the circle until the last person is asked to repeat the message, which is inevitably a gross distortion of the original phrase. The same thing happens in social networks.

People add their own experiences, interpretations, and context to information they receive. Take recruiting practices, for example, in which many managers are involved. This, too, could lead to a cluster of expertise because it deals with a very tightly connected group of people with the same knowledge base. Or, if a group who shares a past comes together, it can be very difficult for an outsider to break into the inner circle. This is an especially common practice in most venture capital and private equity-backed early stage companies.

One of the most impressive aspects of Cross and Parker's research on the hidden power of social networks is their analysis of 60 strategically important networks in a wide range of household name organizations over a five-year period. In areas such as consulting, pharmaceuticals, computer hardware and software, consumer products, financial services, petrochemical, heavy equipment and machinery—and yes, even government—they clearly illustrate the broad-based application of social networks in developing customer, people, and operational world-class environments.

Five Functional Areas Where SNA Can Be Most Applicable

There are five fundamental areas that we believe can greatly benefit from the quantifiable value of business relationships. Each area is driven by Relationship-Centric Goals, heavily influenced by those with a reputation for expertise and responsiveness, and each is instrumental to the short- and long-term success of your business.

1. Business Development

Beyond sales and marketing, which are short-term and tactical, smart companies aim to truly develop business. What I call business development is not only acquiring a strong command of your own core competencies, but also finding the courage to succinctly identify gaps in your current offerings as well as opportunities for exponential scale through other individuals, distribution channels, markets, or more advantageous margin structures. These opportunities can come from unlikely sources and the most efficient way to tap into them is to through as diverse a social network as possible.

As Michael Rene, former chief strategy officer at Choicepoint explains, "It is difficult for large, complex bureaucratic companies to innovate. It is much easier for small, nimble, highly focused niche players to not only improve an existing product, process, or go-to-market strategy, but to also truly come up with marketable innovation." Your access to these pockets of brilliance is exponentially enhanced with a broad-based social network. In the next chapter, I highlight not only sources of value creation, but also key characteristics of business development as transformational in its target market versus the *transactional* nature of sales.

Relationships take time, effort, and investments. The value of these relationships may not show up in this or next quarter's pipeline, but if cultivated correctly, they will create a significant long-term return. The challenge is that most companies, teams, and individuals are not good at building these kinds of quantifiable business-development relationships. To make them successful, you need an organization with unique skill sets, capabilities, and relationship-building styles. Building a strategic relationship plan can drive unparalleled efficiencies in how you share information, transfer critical knowledge, and make long-term, mutually beneficial decisions.

2. Leadership Development

With few exceptions, not enough formalized mentoring occurs in U.S. business today. As the generation before ours retires, these leaders leave a very real void in the next generation of leadership. Today, more executives retire earlier in their careers and take much of their valuable insights and knowledge with them when they go. Key intracompany relationships developed in a formalized mentoring program cannot only enable much of that crucial knowledge transfer, but continue to develop it into world-class processes and competitive differentiators.

A fundamental core competency of a true leader is the ability to gather multiple sources of information, extract insights from that information, make sound decisions, and then effectively communicate those decisions to the diverse makeup of the broader organization. In many companies, managers and leaders are taught to *functionally* become the best they can be—the strategic value of financial stewardship or the value of real-time information from a technology platform—but taught nothing about how to effectively build and leverage relationships across diverse operating groups.

Traditional leadership development that is corporate driven also typically leaves it to the corporation to match the mentor with a mentee. Within social networks, mentees are taught how to broaden their portfolio of relationships and expand that mentoring beyond the formal to the informal. This turns your entire leadership development from a top-down organizational structure to a side-and-out structured model. Effective social networks start from the bottom and move out in every direction.

The key is to build an environment where you move from performance evaluations that are viewed as a *have to do* and instead build personal SWOT (strength, weakness, opportunity, threat) profiles and a formal mentoring program to help key individuals become not just better managers, but better human beings.

Relationship Economics @ Work:
Dale Silvia at Scientific-Atlanta

According to Dale Silvia, VP of HR for Cisco Service Provider Video Technology Group (SPVTG), who leads the group's engineering leadership development program, many mentoring programs are typically an organizationally sponsored, mechanical approach that is limited by formal relationships and partnerships.

"Instead of waiting for the organization to structure a formal program, we teach our people to seek out their mentors and engage those individuals who will help them better understand the areas in which they currently need help," said Silvia. "There is nothing wrong with formal mentoring programs per se, but they can oftentimes be self-limiting. If you give people the know-how, you give them the permission and tools to go get what they need. You are flipping the pyramid upside down and suddenly you have a broad base of people that you can at least informally call your mentoring group. That is two-way sharing."

At SPVTG, newly hired undergrad and graduate engineers participate in an extensive leadership development program that relies heavily on the principles taught in Relationship Economics. Specifically, new hires are taught how to make deposits in relationships so that they can withdraw on them when they need help.

"I take these new graduates, give them direction and the permission to seek out the key people in the organization, and I challenge them to build relationships that will help them and others become more successful over time," said Silvia. "They all come back and tell me what value it produced for them. Over months or years of doing this, you can really see the personal and professional growth."

Silvia's message to the next generation of leaders is clear: "I tell them to go out and become famous for something. Build those relationships in a positive way. Show people what they can do. Go out of your way to help those people and you will have a solid foundation throughout your career because you will have people who want you to succeed."

It comes down to human capital, Silvia claims. It comes down to that personal connection and the perseverance to exercise that over time. Not in a greedy fashion, but in a way that you, those around you, and the entire organization will benefit.

3. Strategy Execution

As I have said before, there is no shortage of strategy formulation. The problem is strategy execution! Every executive with whom we have worked has challenging stories about how the brilliant 400-page strategic analysis of their business—prepared by high-priced consultants—could never be implemented because the company lacks the resources and talent to convert academic exercises into actionable steps.

Public service organizations rely very heavily on their basis of knowledge, which is often gathered through tenure, especially given the current challenges as Baby Boomers make up the largest percentage of the workforce. But over the next five years, many of these Baby Boomers will choose to retire and move to the lake and there simply isn't a replenishable pool of equally talented and knowledgeable workers. In a situation where knowledge is not valued until it begins to cascade through the organization and leak through retirement, it is critical to find a way to map those subject matter experts by their peers. Social Network Analysis can become a useful decision support tool for the planning and execution of these key strategic initiatives.

The questions then become how do you identify critical expertise, how do you map the source of that expertise, and how do you establish a practical knowledge transfer process? The answer is a peer evaluation through parallel queries with each recipient responding by selecting from a list of names. The result is a critical list of key players who can A) help with the development of up and coming key players and B) uncover a number of surprises in key organizational resources.

It is interesting that subjectivity is ultimately reduced with peer evaluations, and the popularity contest inevitably diminishes. As you attempt to identify communities or practices of expertise, you tend to highlight strategic vulnerabilities in critical skill assets that you either need and don't have or those that are few and far between. Through this process, you can identify isolated and highly underused individuals and develop a precisely targeted training and knowledge continuity plan for carrying key strategic initiatives across geographic, functional, and business unit boundaries.

4. Adaptive Innovation of Best Practices

As a new divisional leader, how do you quickly uncover and leverage knowledge, experience, and specific expertise across the disparate parts of your organization in an effort to not only retain your best customers, but also to expand your mind share and wallet share within each of your most profitable client companies? First, map your relationship dynamics chart by learning who individuals go to for information. Who has deeply rooted departmental, divisional, or companywide information specifically focused on getting things done? Don't just map the subject of the content of e-mail exchanges—map the *connections*. Look at who is copied and the frequency of exchanges compared to others in the organization. Beyond a charming personality, who is *functionally* missed when he's not there? With objective information, you can identify not only those who are most connected, but those who collaborate instinctively and as a daily course of performing their functions.

Most of our clients are surprised by this phenomenon, yet it somehow reaffirms their intuition that social networks are often much more valuable than systems or databases of learning and sharing information. Silos, despite efforts by leadership to the contrary, are very much alive and well established within many networks and there are hidden revenue or cost-saving opportunities that could be derived through strategic relationships. Of particular interest to several clients has also been the fact that some of the most connected people are those that rank lower in the company's traditional hierarchy. But as leaders, they are well served to prioritize those relationships because of their influence within the group.

Other defining characteristics of social networks are individual roles including realm of responsibilities, length of time at the firm, current position, and nature of their department of functional role. Innovation should be promoted across the entire organization. It is the quantifiable value of collaborative relationships that fuels innovation. Remember that it is not necessarily the best ideas that rise through the company's bureaucratic ranks and become market leading products and services, but rather the ideas backed by the most influential relationships in the organization.

5. Large-Scale Change and Mergers and Acquisitions

At some point, your three percent organic growth, although perhaps respectable in your industry, will become less than attractive for the organization. As such, the senior leaders or the board may recommend a more aggressive, inorganic growth strategy that encompasses a strong spring of deal flow, preacquisition, due diligence, and postacquisition integration, typically driven by the project management office.

Make no mistake—there is seldom a merger. Instead, there is typically an *acquisition* and often, the integration of disparate employee teams into an expansive geography. Separate functional groups working in different locations drive incredibly inefficient and often dysfunctional redundancies in their implementation of various programs and initiatives.

IT, though a broad-reaching shared service, is often a good but unfortunately painful example of this scenario. Infrastructure, large projects, pockets of unique expertise, mandates by business units, and the critical nature of the organization's operational efficiency based on a consistent and productive IT strategy makes matters worse. After any acquisition, IT leaders often recognize that a reorganization and reprioritization is not only necessary, but critical to seamless continuity. The goal is often to break down us-versus-them silos and get people in Europe, Asia, and the Americas talking to one another not only to improve IT services, but to create efficiencies in the desired output. So, how do you break down silos and get people talking? First, map out social networks of intracompany relationships to reveal who is most overworked, most isolated, and most connected without alienating any particular employee or teams. Then, convey the painfully clear value of collaboration or lack thereof.

You would be amazed at how many people are disconnected across functional lines by physical distances or even with those working on key projects. Some are to be expected, but others can cause enormous pain and redundancy in an organization. Often, reorganization is needed based on functional groups as opposed to teams of experts. For example, if the enterprise resource planning deployment team does not fully understand the critical steps in the process, nor do they develop the relationships with the frontline users of that technology to extract candor regarding what is really broken and how to fix the process before implementing the technology, the implementation is sure to fail.

Many cross-functional social networks often become enablers to more effective communication and unity in their respective parts of the bigger picture. Geography creates a very real disconnect, which team-building sessions can help overcome. Last, strategic knowledge communities in areas such as project management, process reengineering and client services previously unknown to the senior staff, can emerge.

5

Relationship-Centric Goals for Business Development

In Chapter 1, I mentioned that most traditional networking is often deemed ineffective because of a lack of relationship-centric goals. These are business goals that a team, individual, or organization simply cannot achieve without a systematic and disciplined focus on their most valuable relationships. In this chapter, I examine the most prevalent area for the quantifiable outcome of relationships: business development. Notice that I didn't say sales and marketing. If sales is the infantry, think of strategic business development as the Navy Seals. It should further quantifiably reduce your customer acquisition costs, help expand your current market reach across multiple markets, or help segment your access deeper and wider in your current markets. Here, I address how to establish equity relationship-centric goals for the purpose of business development—particularly for nonbusiness developers.

Fundamental Difference between Brand Awareness and Business Development

Product-centric companies are forced to effectively delineate their unique differentiators. Unfortunately, professional services organizations such as the Big Four accounting firms—as well as a multitude of law firms, engineering, and construction companies—also struggle with the same challenge. For example, how are the legal services of one international law firm really different from those of another? Although many such organizations attempt to highlight the breadth and depth of their talents, unique set of processes, and successful past engagements that contribute to the broad-based experiences—they all have the same basic ingredients. It is the savvy professional service organizations that realize the orchestration of relationship assets at a multitude of business stature levels and geographic locations is what really sets them apart.

Your overall revenue generation engine has many interdisciplinary activities at work that all drive toward a common cause. They must operate as a cohesive function of your organization and create forward motion. The revenue generation engine focuses on customer and market acquisition and retention and includes two main components: the pretransaction phase before they become customers and the posttransaction sale after they've chosen to invest in you, your brand, firm, or value promised. It is amazing how often individuals, teams, and organizations take the posttransaction element for granted. Let's take a look at each of these stages:

Before They Become Customers

Within customer acquisition, relationships are the fundamental enablers or drivers in several key areas. It is important to remember that relationships are not a substitute for performance—rather, they are complementary to it. In fact, performance trumps all. To be successful, you have to begin with a product or service that performs superbly in the market. Once you have a strong core product or service, it is very easy to build around it.

I have never known a business that can survive without performance. If you are an environmental consulting company and you can't provide accurate audits, you won't stay in business long. Dell was initially known for its simplified product mix and mostly positive end-user support experiences. However, when the product mix became entirely too complex (do we really need 30 different laptop models?) and its quality of support diminished, both its reputation and market share dramatically weakened. Even the dry cleaner around the corner from my house will lose my vote of confidence and subsequent business if it can't meet my expectations, as well as my *preferences* (medium starch on hangers) consistently. At its core, your product or service has to perform. Once you have that in place, relationships can greatly aid that revenue generator.

It has been said that, "Nothing ever happens until someone, somewhere, sells something." Beyond its complexity and evolution over the years, any success in sales remains a very relationship-centric function. Though people buy from people they like, trust, and respect, sales often has a very transactional nature about it. A purchase order or invoice is made up of a document and *transaction* that solves an immediate problem. This is not to be confused by the campaign, which must be developed to create the sale, but at the end of the day, we define sales as very transactional.

In contrast, business development *transforms* an organization and creates longer impact. What is transactional in sales can become transformational in business development. Take the Big Four accounting firms: Deloitte, Ernst & Young, KPMG, and PriceWaterhouseCoopers, for example. Most are multifaceted with tax, audit, and advisory services. Tax and audit can be transactional. But advisory services, dealing with financial, long-term consulting, and often strategic issues, are perceived to be highly transformational.

Many companies could greatly benefit from strategic business development. Think of it in terms of parallel swimming lanes. The fundamental difference between branding (air cover), sales (transactional), and strategic business development (transformational) is that business development is long-term and designed to enhance your current market position, extend your market reach, or create new opportunities altogether.

Relationship Economics @ Work: David Goldsmith of MetaMatrix on the Seven Unique Types of Alliances

David Goldsmith, a colleague from the National Speakers Association (NSA) and president and co-founder of New York-based MetaMatrix Consulting Group, has defined seven kinds of alliance relationships—all contributors to your personal and professional success. In all my work with

(*continued*)

Relationship Economics @ Work: David Goldsmith of MetaMatrix on the Seven Unique Types of Alliances (Continued)

decision makers, I find it important that everyone know up front what type of relationship is being developed early on in the game. This common language, drawn from a variety of sources, makes progress happen fast.

1. *Affiliate Relationship*—A partnership that allows two parties to work together with minimal risk to either party. For example, one company may promote another one on their web site where both parties have a limited investment and risk in the relationship.

2. *Ad-hoc Relationship*—A type of relationship that is normally formed for the purposes of solving or looking into a particular challenge. In politics, for instance, you'll hear that an ad hoc committee has been established to review the need for a new sewage plant.

3. *Consortium*—This occurs when a group of people combine their resources, enabling them to achieve significantly more than any individual could do by herself. Associations and chambers of commerce are a very well known type of consortium. Each member contributes just a few dollars per year and in return they receive the benefits of all the funds provided by the members.

4. *Project Joint Venture*—A project joint venture is a relationship in which two parties agree to work together in such a manner that resources from both parties are used, but on a limited scale. The hiring of a printer to print a brochure or when two parties put on an event are examples of such a relationship.

5. *Joint Venture*—This type of relationship requires that both parties commit to working together to the degree

that if one fails, the other fails, and if successful, they both partake in the reward.

6. *Merger*—A merger is when two parties agree that joining together as one would be better for everyone involved and the combined efforts would produce more than each one could individually.

7. *Acquisition*—An acquisition is substantially different from a merger in that in an acquisition one party believes that the relationship would be best for both when joined even if the other disagrees.

When an organization or an individual looks to develop a relationship, it's extremely important that both – or all – parties understand what's actually trying to be achieved. Mistakes are avoided and the desired outcomes are achieved at an accelerated pace by defining what each organization desires early on in the dialog. Think about it this way: If you see a marriage as a joint venture but your partner sees it as a project joint venture . . . well, you're in for trouble.

In the revenue generation engine, successful business development requires the most astute capitalization of strategic relationships. Channel or distribution partners in domestic, or particularly in international, markets must become an extension of your reach, yet consistently convey your unique value proposition. That arm's length reach in the market alters your direct contribution to one of success through influence, often without authority. Only by arming your partner with the appropriate resources and a succinct and accelerated path to incremental and profitable revenue growth will you be able to develop a channel-friendly organization.

One of the best in the technology business development arenas is my good friend and long-term colleague, Charles Daniels, formerly of SGI (Silicon Graphics). Charles and I joined SGI a week apart back in the early 1990s. I was responsible for several named accounts, while Charles masterfully and proactively managed the SGI channel program. His calm, yet results-driven demeanor, high touch and high care personal characteristics, and professional attributes made him—as a direct sales rep, as well as with his channel partners—an absolute joy to work with.

In every opportunity, Charles was a consummate diplomat – not only in creating win-win-win opportunities between the SGI sales force, channel partners, and ultimately the end customers— but by excelling in a multitude of roles, including that of a catalyst, a mediator, an enforcer, and certainly an influencer. The results of Charles's strategic relationship management efforts can only be described as exemplary, as evidenced by his nine trips to the coveted Presidents Club, composed of the most elite 10 percent to 15 percent of the entire SGI sales force.

Relationship-Centric Best Practice: Feet on the Street

Nothing will ever replace feet on the street.

Develop the necessary processes, acquire channel-centric talents, and proactively invest in your most valuable channel relationships because they can drive an estimated 20 percent to 40 percent of your overall revenues at a fraction of your SG&A expenses.

Raj Batra, VP and general manager of the Automation and Motion Division (AMD) and Reiner Pallmann, VP and general manager of the Process Solutions Division (PSD) within Siemens Energy and Automation, lead strategic solution platform for customers in diverse industries such as machine tools, production machines, discrete automation, postal automation, and fluid and gas flow. By strategically investing in a broad-based portfolio of channel relationships, Raj, Reiner, and their respective teams are able to focus on key industry trends such as safety and security, industrial networks, modernization, tracking and tracing, and last but certainly not least, energy and environment.

In the process, by being present at the street level with current and prospective customers and external key market influencers, they continue to perform at an exceptional level. This market presence enables Raj, Reiner, and their teams to engage a network that is much wider and richer than what they could reach on their own.

After They Become Customers

An often undervalued, undermined, and certainly underdeveloped part of an organization is often the postsale part of the revenue generation engine. Many struggle to automatically throw a customer, which they have worked so hard to acquire, over the wall to a customer service department.

The truth is that the real selling begins *after* the sale. It is my belief that quality, customer service, client service, and account management should seldom be a department, but rather a fundamental mindset of the entire organization. A recent survey highlighted that, on average, you have a one-to-two chance of earning incremental business from existing or past clients and a 1-to-18 to 1-to-30 chance, depending on the industry, average sales cycle, and average sales price, in winning that business from a prospect unfamiliar with your past performance.

Your relationships and ability to systematically nurture and keep your finger on the pulse of that customer voice becomes a quantifiable return on integration. By seamlessly incorporating the pre- and postsales functions of the revenue generation engine, you further establish greater barriers of entry by key competitors and sustain a diligent client protection strategy in the process.

If you look at Figure 5.1, it illustrates an outbreak strategy where the X-axis represents your existing products and services and the Y-axis represents your existing customers and distribution channels. Each end of this 2 × 2 matrix represents *existing* and *new*, respectively.

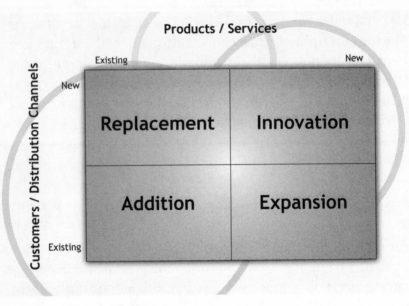

FIGURE 5.1 Up-sell—Cross-sell Matrix.

The easiest thing to sell is more of the same products and services to the exact same customer base. We call that *addition*. Next are your *expansion* strategies, which include selling new products and services to your existing customer base. And by far the most challenging business development cycle tends to be selling new products or services to new customers or channels— what we call *innovation*.

For the bottom two—addition and expansion—functional relationships (as defined in Chapter 1) will suffice. Ideally, many unknown risks have been mitigated through their previous interactions, which have established trust with you, your firm, and the performance of your products and services. Examples of these functional relationships are operations managers or purchasing agents.

The top two—replacement and innovation—will demand strategic relationships to influence at the executive or perhaps even the board level. At this stage, the conversation is greatly elevated from the *what* and *how* to the *why*. Strategic relationships also demand a reduced sense of self-interest and heightened level of strategic problem solving and strategy execution.

Why Many Accountants, Lawyers, Consultants, and Engineers Struggle in this Area

As evidenced by our work with a broad base of professional services clients, many technical professionals are often terrible at selling themselves. Many accountants, attorneys, consultants, and engineers don't think of themselves as salespeople—and they don't want to! Their DNA, through their academic and educational foundation and their professional development, seldom includes the notion of strategic relationships and business development best practices.

I genuinely believe that a very small number of people are born with these best practices and insights into what works. Very few companies and learning and development organizations bring a disciplined approach to the knowledge, skills, and evolutionary development of revenue-generating skills for nonbusiness development professionals.

Relationship-Centric Best Practice: Follow The Money

If you want to know someone's motivation, follow the money. In 9 out of 10 professional services organizations, performance evaluations and compensation plans are not congruent with the needs and desires of the leadership team to drive sales and revenue. Even the word *sales* is seen as or thought of as derogatory and somehow demeaning and beneath their professional accreditation. Yet if you consistently look at individuals who become partners in law firms or senior leaders in these professional service firms—they unequivocally deliver not only exceptional service, but are also able to attract and retain a consistent book of business.

Many people in the accounting and engineering professions, for example, are not typically extroverts: It's just not in their DNA. They are not the relationship-initiating types. Many would rather dive into 400 pages of Sarbanes-Oxley compliance papers or endless technical specifications than attend a networking event where they have to shake hands and exchange business cards.

Additionally, such interaction simply was not part of their education. Networking and relationship-building is not taught in our schools. It isn't part of the accounting or finance curriculum, and it isn't covered by companies upon employment. Law firms seldom teach strategic relationships, and when they do, it is often focused on the *art*. They encourage associates and partners alike to immerse themselves in various civic, professional, and community organizations, yet very few are able to convert relationship creation into relationship capitalization or monetization.

If you can change the perception of transactional, quick-hit sales to a more strategic, longer-term perspective of business development, this competent group of professional service providers will not only listen, but they will embrace practical, pragmatic advice in building and profitably nurturing their respective businesses. By the way, it has been our experience that this group is very good at building relationships based on competency and trust. The challenge often remains creating the initial access and nurturing relationships to extend and expand current engagements.

Flaws in Professional Certification Processes

If you look at many of the professional certification processes such as those required for a CPA, attorney, project managers, and even the medical profession, their curriculum for accreditation seldom includes content focused on the systematic disciplined process for the development of strategic business relationships.

None of these processes motivate, encourage, or praise individuals for the art and science of building, nurturing, and leveraging relationships. Instead, and rightfully so, they credit ethics, operational efficiency, and HR policies. They applaud continuing education in compliance, but frown upon the very essence of their survival and success, which is business development and building strategic and quantifiable relationships.

And when it comes to compensation, whatever is spent comes directly out of the partners' pockets, so asking them to dedicate resources to building their business development skills is often frowned upon as unnecessary. Or, they hire rainmakers—people who have networking in their DNA—to drive revenue for them. But these people are few and far between and can provide a false sense of security. For example, if a power networker brings a huge international deal to a firm that keeps 20 people busy for two years, the firm may be led to believe that it is succeeding—but how will they develop 10 more of these types of deals?

Competency and Trust as Critical Components of Reputation Capital

As mentioned earlier, as you promote value and deliver it, you begin to exchange Relationship Currency. And as the delivery of that value is recognized, you start to accumulate *reputation capital*. The two fundamental pillars of Reputation Capital are competency and trust.

Competency

Strategic business development involves a multitude of constituents and partners, and your success heavily depends on competency. Any alliance partner you engage with will ask, *Where else have you done this? Where have you been successful with this project, team, individual, and organization?* So that you are prepared to answer these questions, perform your own competency assessment to quickly gauge what your fundamental product and service strengths are. Clearly define your current state (where you are today), and a future state (where you aspire to reach). The difference becomes your developmental gap. This level of competency assessment creates a road map for personal and professional development.

Relationship-Centric Best Practice: Client-Centric Teams

An extremely positive trend in many professional service firms is the breaking down of the traditional functional, geographic, and expertise-centric silos to one of a matrix organization with client-centric teams. Having gone through this process, prominent Atlanta law firm Alston + Bird was able to create a client team encompassing a multitude of legal disciplines for one of its major clients. By using its global talent, they were able to overlay client teams over their usual functions (legal, real estate, accounting, and so forth) to solve the client's issues and exponentially increase their billable fees. This client-centric focus makes relationships both inside the law firm, as well as outside it, that much more productive. Today, the firm has more than 30 similar client teams in place.

Similarly, for years, PriceWaterhouseCoopers has had a client relationship partner on site at large accounts such as Home Depot with a partner serving as the quarterback and orchestrating the firm's global resources to deliver its exceptional expertise to Home Depot's unique challenges and opportunities.

Remember: Value creation is derived from value-chain disruption. If you don't disrupt your market, customers, and suppliers—your competitors will!

Trust

Think of the concept of a *trust barometer*. If I am one of your channel or distribution partners, for example, you are asking me to put my reputation on the line to walk you into my end customers. That is huge on the trust barometer. Components of that trust start in an organization, but often come down to trust between individuals. We all start out with a certain level of credibility and, over time, can choose to either enhance, reinforce, and cement that credibility by consistently executing and delivering on promises made, or we can choose to dilute it by incongruence and inconsistency between your thought, words and actions.

Trust, as an outcome of your competency simply defined, is predictability in what you say and do on a consistent basis over an extended period of time. The challenge with trust is that it takes years to develop and moments to destroy. Individuals, teams, and organizations have to make it their lifelong focus and mission to establish and protect their position on their trust barometer. And that trust barometer is applicable to a whole host of constituents. Take employees, for example. The first time you lie to me as a boss, I won't trust you again. The first time you mess with my expenses or break our contract, you have diluted that credibility and broken that trust. Conversely, if you are consistently candid and forthcoming and you foreshadow that which others should expect from you, you can build and solidify this fundamental pillar called trust.

Relationship-Centric Goals

As we discussed at the beginning of the book, most traditional networking fails because it is practiced without a purpose, goal, or plan. Whether that goal is client acquisition and retention, finding the next job or buying a company—relationship-centric goals are those in which you need others to help you achieve. Specifically, these are business relationships with colleagues, clients, suppliers, media, analysts, and the business community at large. There are three types of relationship-centric goals.

Direct Goals

Direct goals are black and white goals that are clear, simple to understand, and to the point. They are quantifiable, directly related to how you are measured, and generally on the 12-to-18-month horizon.

Examples
- Buy a $20 million discrete manufacturing company in Atlanta this fiscal year.
- Transfer internally to the New Hotel Opening Team by mid-July.
- Find a new marketing job in the consumer brands industry by January 1.

Influence Goals

These are goals over which you have less personal control in achieving. They often require other things to fall in place on your behalf, such as the influence of others. To achieve these goals, you will have to influence key situations or align your efforts with key influencers in the organization. When setting these types of goals, go beyond your comfort zone. What do you want to achieve 18 to 36 months from now? How will you know when you've arrived?

Examples
- Expand my portfolio of political relationships by four new members this calendar year.
- Achieve an 8 out of 10 customer satisfaction rating on the next survey.

- Earn 20 percent to 40 percent of new business from key European markets by the middle of next year.

Equity Goals

Equity goals are often intangible and difficult to quantify. These include areas such as branding and building a go-to person reputation or increased market awareness. What positive things do you want people to say about you? What is your personal brand? What are you doing to research, package, build, and market your brand for more responsibility and positive visibility within the firm and the community in which you live and work? If you look back three to five years from now, what will you have accomplished?

Examples
- Establish a go-to person reputation for connecting entrepreneurs with capital
- Develop a reputation in my department as the one who really gets it, has great follow-through, and is extremely driven.
- Create a reputation of having one of the highest personal integrities in the mergers and acquistions business.

The Challenges

Goals are fundamentally more achievable if they are written down and reviewed. For goals to be effective, they must also be quantifiable and have a time frame. Remember that if you can't measure it, you're unlikely to track your progress and you won't be able to make course corrections along the way.

It is also critical to filter your goals for realism. Next time you write down a goal, ask yourself these three questions:

1. *Are your goals realistic?* Even clearly defined, fact-based goals can be frustrating to pursue if they are not realistic. Don't

---

Relationship-Centric Best Practice: Daily View of Your Goals

Sit down, find some quiet time, and really think about the specific, quantifiable goals you want to achieve. I've taped mine to my bathroom mirror so that every morning when I get up to get ready for work, I know where I'm going, what I'll do when I get there, and what I am aiming to achieve.

---

confuse achievable or the need to push oneself with what is truly attainable.

2. *Are they achievable within your sphere of influence and control?* What other factors contribute to the attainability of your goal? Is your goal dependent on things outside of your control or influence?

3. *Are they documented, measured, and analyzed along a defined time line?* Goals must be consistently documented, measured, analyzed, and appropriately responded to along the way. If the goal is not documented and if quantifiable metrics and time lines are not identified, how will you measure your progress against them? If you don't measure your progress, how will you analyze what's working and what's not with each relationship? If you don't analyze effectiveness, how can you make any course corrections in your relationship investment strategy and tactical execution?

6

Pivotal Contacts for Leadership Development

Most leadership development programs are very myopic in their approach. They train high-performing managers on how to become the best in their functional roles, yet they underemphasize the most central issue of fundamental and lasting leadership: the ability to engage an increasingly diverse workforce with generations of deep-rooted beliefs, expectations, and pet peeves. Beyond cultural diversity, pivotal contacts are key individuals who can accelerate one's ability to achieve key goals, strategies, objectives, and tactics (GSOT). In this chapter, I quantify accelerated execution, give succinct examples of sources of pivotal contacts, highlight *hubs and spokes,* illustrate sample profiles, and review a scorecard of how to identify your most valuable pivotal contacts.

Myopia in Leadership Development

Typically, our view of leadership development encompasses the escalation of current high performers into an environment where they can develop a broader set of competencies and capabilities. In many organizations, the senior leaders aim to manage the perception of the issues, form coalitions, and use relationships to influence change in the organization. Without "relationships and influence," they are without arrows in their managerial quiver. In our experience, however, we have found that many leadership development programs fail to include the quantifiable and strategic value of business relationships—not only as another bucket or segment of the curriculum, but also as part of the encompassing framework in the development of the next generation of corporate leaders. In other words, you could be the most astute financial leader, operations leader, manufacturing executive or complex project owner, but if you lack the ability to proactively and systematically identify, build, and nurture personal, functional, and strategic relationships to influence others, I am not convinced of your fully realized long-term success in any organization.

According to former SunTrust executive Dan Brown, "[little] *l* leadership typically focuses downward. I have four managers reporting to me and they have 20 people each reporting to them. Though this type of leadership plays an important role, it typically focuses on accomplishing something you are doing as a team. Big *L* leadership deals with influence. How am I working with my peers and people above me? How do I formulate a coalition with this person, or this person? It usually doesn't take as much time to formulate a relationship or influence . . . people at lower levels. But once you create that influence above, you really become a leader.

"When I was at SunTrust, I had a project that wasn't going well. A subordinate in rank who worked for another manager asked me about it. After I explained the situation, he said, I can help you get that done. It's stuck and one of my peers is holding it up. I'll fix that. I have a relationship with that person. I will fix that and it will help you and it will help us all around.

"I started taking him to lunch once a quarter. This was obviously a person in the business who could break down barriers and get things done. He could generate solutions for people outside of his group," Dan added.

The increasing diversity of today's workforce makes it that much more critical that our future leaders can effectively engage those who don't look, sound, or think like us and lead them toward a common set of strategic goals and objectives. In addition to providing cultural diversity, key individuals with unique perspectives and insights can accelerate any leader's ability to achieve results. We call these people *Pivotal Contacts*.

In researching dozens of Fortune 500 leadership development programs, we found many to be myopic in their perspective and focused purely on safe topics such as strategy, financial engineering, and global expansion. Many try to elevate your thinking, executing from the purely tactical (*what* we are doing) to the more strategic (*why* we are doing this). Then there is the holistic approach that questions not just the ability, but the social responsibility aspects as well. Although extremely beneficial to current high performers and those perceived to be high potentials, these questions don't include a systematic, disciplined approach to functional and strategic relationships.

Strategic relationships are seldom part of any personal evaluations we have reviewed to date. Nor are they part of any compensation model we have seen, at least no compensation plan that actually moves one's needle (a 5 percent variable is not really an incentive). They are not part of a human resource organization's competency maps, nor formal mentoring programs aimed at raising the bar on key functional leaders today. Unless the appropriate metrics and rewards are in place to accurately align the organization's goals and objectives with that of the individual in a highly relationship-centric environment, how will we overcome this fundamental and often myopic perspective of world-class leadership development programs?

Relationship-Centric Best Practice: Politically Savvy

Take a look at the following excerpts from world-class leadership development programs. The foreword asks:

- How do you know when your team is winning? How do you know when they are losing?
- What do you look for in a leader?
- What questions do you ask to separate the high performing and high potentials?
- Why has your team been successful?

(continued)

Relationship-Centric Best Practice:
Politically Savvy (Continued)

Throughout close to 400 pages of concepts, case studies, exercises, and reviews, the notion of business relationships as a strategic asset is mentioned in less than a single paragraph. We exert a great deal of energy developing a strategic mindset, constructing plans, and investing in field execution, yet many simply do not believe that corporate politics is worthy of their attention.

I am often reminded of Plato, who said, *"Those who are too smart to engage in politics are usually punished by being governed by those considerably dumber than themselves."* Become astute in describing the motivation and key forces in human nature and organizational structures, which make the political system both necessary and unavoidable. Not only are there political structures in every organization, but they tend to be highly influenced by a select group of insider relationships. Their key lieutenants, both formal and informal within the organization, as well as key external advisers, can provide unparalleled access to opportunities with those who have invested in deep and broad-based relationships. Only by establishing personal credibility and direct or indirect business value to those in highly influential roles will you be able to formulate a professional, polished, and ethical win-win solution for long-term viability and success within your organization.

Inclusion as a Strategic Asset

Though many forward thinking companies have a diversity initiative—a change initiative that specifically addresses the core dimensions of differences or an initiative to improve workplace conditions—few really talk about relationship diversity and what goes on every day under the radar. Diversity has to be understood as more than affirmative action. Diversity is about trust, respect, and productivity. Relationships can often power and elevate these three elements through inclusion of unique perspectives and independent insights. Innovation is accelerated to shorten time to market; personnel acquisition costs and the cost of a bad hire are reduced; and a very distinct and quantifiable differentiation is created between strategic execution and yet another corporate agenda.

I am reminded of a mentor of mine who once said, "Each of us, having walked a very distinct path, could get us where we are today." When brought together around a common cause, we also bring very different understandings, experiences, and unique capabilities to view the same set of challenges and opportunities. In essence, we are the products of the advice we have taken over the years and our past influences often solidify or frame our recommendations in the future. The more diverse those experiences, the more inclusive of a broad-based set of constituents and the more likely a successful outcome of any challenge or struggle.

Diversify Your Portfolio of Relationships

Your personal and professional success depends on the diversity and quality of your relationships with others, yet most of us don't spend enough time building and nurturing the key relationships we need to achieve success. Many times, we neglect to build relationships outside of our comfort zones with qualified co-workers and employees, ensuring that everyone in the talent pool has access to mentoring and coaching opportunities to grow professionally.

Personal relationships aim to enhance personal and professional development and are often utilized for referral of useful information and contacts. They are mostly externally focused on current and future potential and encompass discretionary contacts with a sense of uncertainty regarding those most relevant. Personal relationships garner their value in the breadth of the network by reaching out to contacts who can make referrals. Think of the last time you searched for a medical specialist. Many will comb their friends for appropriate referrals.

Functional relationships are driven by efficiency. By maintaining capacity and functions required of the group, they are mostly internally focused and are interest oriented. Key contacts are relatively nondiscretionary; the members are prescribed by tasks and organizational structures, and adding others is very clear to those most relevant. Functional networks gain their value in *depth*, focusing primarily on building working relationships. Think of the last time you were looking for someone to help optimize your SAP implementation or your search for a Six Sigma black belt. You combed your functional relationships and reached out to the most relevant subject matter expert.

Strategic relationships aim to uncover future challenges and opportunities. They require support from a highly diverse and influential pool of stakeholders. They are within and external to the organization and focused towards the future, where key contacts flow from strategic context. Membership is extremely discretionary and strength is gained by creating a hybrid of internal and external assets. Think of mergers and acquisitions or international expansion. Many of the individuals you may know today could simply be irrelevant in those efforts.

Pivotal Contacts

Certain individuals can help accelerate your ability to achieve your goals. Not just meet your goals, because many people can get there by themselves, but truly *accelerate* your achievement of them. For example, it might take you six months on your own to reach the CEO of Company X to offer your suggestions on how to accelerate his Asia-Pacific revenue growth. Or, instead, the CFO of that same company could personally walk you into the CEO's office in less than two weeks. That is accelerated access and it can be obtained by knowing the right people, or those whom we call *Pivotal Contacts.*

Pivotal Contacts are thought leaders among their peers. They have developed deep subject matter expertise, have proven themselves in situations requiring a balanced approach between strategic vision and tactical execution, or simply have access to influential relationships. They are commonly referred to as movers and shakers in a given role, company, vertical industry, or city. They are rising stars and key influencers, and often lead the most critical projects within any company. They are highly thought of in board meetings, mentioned in industry trade publications, and make numerous appearances in industry forums. They are always invited to speak at the company's offsite strategy session or cross-industry conferences for their unique best practices. They are published writers, authors, or subject matter authorities, and are considered pillars of their organization or industry.

Relationship-Centric Best Practice: "Most Influential"

Google "most influential 40 under 40," and you're likely to find pivotal contacts that someone, somewhere, has already sought out. The *Inc.* 500, the *Training* magazine Top 150, and yes, even the "ten most influential players in the concrete industry" are all examples of those who, in many ways, have seen the movie and suffered through the pitfalls you're headed for.

Yet many look at such lists and simply think to themselves, "That's nice." They often ignore these gold mines of industry, geography, or subject matter insiders. Proactively seek out the people on these lists. Find value-based reasons to get introduced to them and, more important, become an asset to them. These individuals will exponentially increase your visibility, level of access, and perceived influence in your desired market.

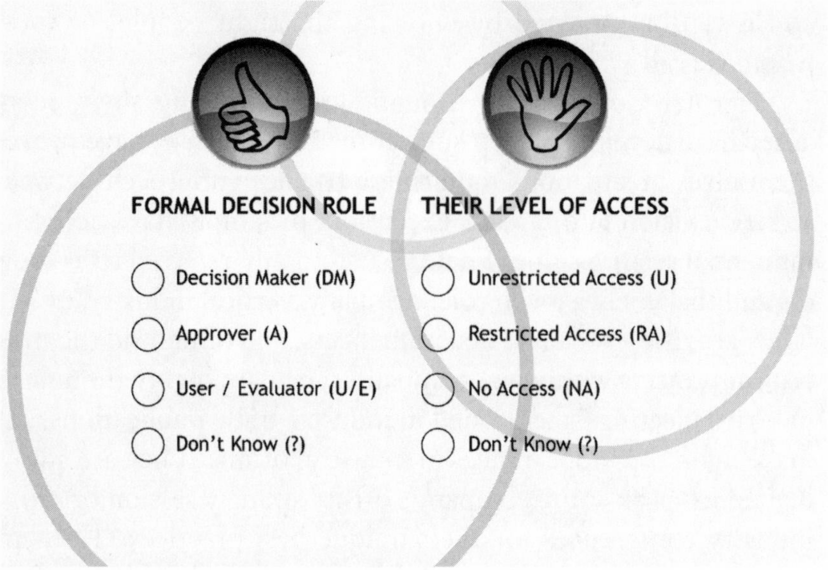

FORMAL DECISION ROLE

- ◯ Decision Maker (DM)
- ◯ Approver (A)
- ◯ User / Evaluator (U/E)
- ◯ Don't Know (?)

THEIR LEVEL OF ACCESS

- ◯ Unrestricted Access (U)
- ◯ Restricted Access (RA)
- ◯ No Access (NA)
- ◯ Don't Know (?)

FIGURE 6.1   Pivotal Contact Attributes.

Regardless of any particular function you currently serve or aspire to reach, a pivotal contact's formal decision role tells you a great deal about their business stature. Of particular interest are the two critical areas: their formal decision role and level of access. (See Figure 6.1.) Their formal decision role is one of the following.

Decision Maker

Most decision makers I know, whether entrepreneurs in a company of five employees or CEO of a multibillion dollar global corporation, didn't get there overnight. By consistently practicing the ability and willingness to make decisions, they have gained a great deal of experience in evaluating highly dynamic choices—as well as risk potentials—in transactions, and with the right individuals.

Mark Jowell, CEO of LogicJunction (a leading developer of avatars capable of engaging a broad-based audience in retail, customer service, product marketing, and even a gracious event host) has learned how to prioritize critical relationships both inside and outside his growth-oriented venture. Years ago, I introduced Mark to Peter Augusta, a former SGI colleague who in recent years had specialized in the retail industry. In many ways, Peter has been instrumental to Mark's success in this market. His ability to make the decision to invest in Peter and his portfolio of relationships make this access to a pivotal contact highly quantifiable, and strategically viable to the success of the business.

Approver

In my experience, these are highly valued lieutenants. Convince them of your value-based relationship approach and you'll fast track your access to the Decision Maker.

I was introduced to David Grucza, director of strategy and business development for the Process Solutions division at Siemens Energy and Automation, through a mutual friend who had heard a keynote on Relationship Economics. From our first meeting over two years ago, David was naturally inquisitive, professionally astute, and collaborative with an outsider's potential value-add to not only his division, but equally important, as an asset to his VP and divisional GM, Reiner Pallmann.

David took the time to clearly understand that a group of highly diverse business units executing in a more relationship-centric environment would create a very sustainable differentiation for the PSD team. He approved our joint game plan and was instrumental in getting the initial buy-in from Reiner. It didn't hurt that David had earned Reiner's respect and trust and that Reiner himself also saw the value of not simply a technically superior solution, but also one that could greatly benefit from an elevated sense of mutual trust, respect, and admiration.

User Evaluator

It is critical to walk a fine line here. Ignore this group and they have the potential to become cancerous in your efforts to achieve critical mass of valuable relationships. Aim to develop a highly cordial and engaging relationship with those who will ultimately put your value proposition to the test.

Early in my career, I witnessed the exponential rise of a certain engineering software company. Their sales model was one of recruiting highly assertive salespeople who were extremely aggressive, outright pushy, abrasive, and who operated with a "buy from us or we'll go over your head" mentality. If the evaluation of their software was in any way jeopardized by the engineering manager's Bowling Night conflicts, they wouldn't think twice about going over his head and the VP of engineering's to reach the company president and get a deal signed.

Needless to say, this company—largely due to a sheer ignorance or dismissal of emotional and social intelligence—alienated a great number of users and evaluators. Even though they were often successful in their customer acquisition campaigns, in countless accounts, the retaliation of the user community led to their ultimate demise.

Don't Know

It is actually okay not to know a pivotal contact's formal decision role, but it is dangerous to assume without verifying. One of the worst things you can do is invest in the wrong relationships. This is not to say that you should be manipulative or only spend time with those from whom you can benefit. It is simply to say that you don't have the ability to invest in everyone equally. It is critical that you succinctly identify the key attributes of contacts that you will find most helpful. Assume a 5 percent differential in your pivotal contact's formal decision role and we've proven a 22 percent detriment in lost time, effort, and valuable resources in various projects, business development campaigns, go-to-market initiatives, or customer retention and expansion strategies.

Sources of Pivotal Contacts: Hubs and Spokes

Pivotal contacts are also often hubs in their chosen fields. Here are some other common traits:

Time—To pivotal contacts, *time* is a valuable asset and they don't like to waste it. You're not likely to see these people hanging out by the water cooler, chatting it up.

Execution—Pivotal contacts are passionate about *execution.* Seldom will they get excited about a 100-page analysis of a challenge. They are much less interested in everything you know and much more intrigued by what they need to know to get things done.

Gatekeepers—Pivotal contacts are protected by very capable *gatekeepers.* The old days of the cliché secretary are long gone. Today's executive administrators and administrative assistants are polished, well-educated, professional, well-paid, and very good at what they do. They take pride in being professional administrators and are focused on optimizing their executives' valuable resources.

Mutual Trust, Respect, and Value—Pivotal contacts build relationships based on *mutual trust, respect, and value.* Often, the only source of access is through a referral by a trusted source. These include lieutenants inside the organization or highly-valued external advisers, but certainly those who have filtered out the time or resource wasters.

Private—It has been my experience that pivotal contacts are well-known, yet *private* individuals. You may hear of their accomplishments, but seldom about their personal lives—including their family matters, political views, or downtime interests.

Pivotal contacts are often one to two business stature levels above your current perceived reach. If you are a manager, for example, a pivotal contact could be a vice president. If you are a director, they could be division presidents. If you are a senior executive, pivotal contacts could include the CEO, board of directors, or SVP of the parent company. Pivotal contacts can also be peers in other departments or of higher stature in other organizations such as private equity firms.

The other critical attribute of a pivotal contact is their level of access. How well are they known, respected, and trusted? Are they perceived to be of quantifiable value? If not regarded highly, their access will be extremely limited. A pivotal contact's level of access can be categorized in four distinct areas.

Unrestricted Access

Meet almost any chief strategy officer, astute executive in investor relations, strategic general counsel, or those few in human resources who can align business strategy with investing in an organization's human capital and you'll quickly recognize their unfettered and unrestricted access. While many complain about not having a seat at the table, the roles characterized here earned that seat through exemplary performance in their respective functions and their canny ability to quickly assess opportunities and risk and communicate critical matters to the appropriate executives.

Restricted Access

Restricted access could be due to a functional role such as that of product engineer, which doesn't necessarily lend itself to private conversations with a CEO. This could also include geographic limitations—a remote office in Albuquerque, New Mexico, has trouble accessing executives at the corporate office in downtown Manhattan.

New members of an organization may have restricted access because they haven't earned their stripes or don't yet have the proper professional maturity. Or, perhaps they have stumbled in the past and have lost their access because they abused it and broke someone's trust. In some cases, an individual's access is limited because their superiors are potentially threatened or annoyed by them.

It is critical to understand *why* a pivotal contact's access is restricted because there are certain reasons—like experience—that can be made up for and others that are truly insurmountable.

No Access

This is another group not to be ignored because they can often be a great source of firsthand knowledge and insights at the street-level rank and file. This group is often passionate about their contributions, and their lack of access could be easily overlooked with a high degree of domain expertise. Think of that frontline project manager or engineer or that first-year associate out of law school.

Don't Know

See the section on formal decision roles. The same issues absolutely apply. Remember: It's okay to not know—but assume to have access and pursue that pivotal contact and you will waste a lot of cycles and resources.

Relationship-Centric Best Practice: Diversity as a Strategic Asset

Sit down with your list of relationship-centric goals. Pick one goal and identify as many diverse buckets of people as you can who could be instrumental to your success. Then, for each bucket, write down specific names of individuals and why you think they could be relevant.

For an example of the "bucket" exercise, take the goal: *I want to buy a $20 million discrete manufacturing company in Mexico City by December 31.* Diverse categories of pivotal contacts instrumental to your success would include sources of deal flow and creative financing, fulfilling gaps in your management team, and building a board of directors or advisers. Sources for these functions could include:

- *Attorneys.* Not just any law firm, but one that specializes in mid-market mergers and acquisitions. And not just any attorney at that firm, but ideally the firm's managing partner. Managing partners are one to two business stature levels higher than someone you can reach on your own and they often have a broader perspective into the ongoing activities, efforts, and key relationships of the firm.
- *Accountants.* Build a relationship with a managing partner of a firm that does the audit and tax work for this vertical market (same reason as above).
- *Consultants, Marketers, and other Strategic Service Providers.* You would be surprised to learn the breadth and depth of the types of deals these folks see on a daily basis.
- *Retained Search Executives.* These people are in the human capital business and have very broad portfolios of relationships. The good ones have unbelievable access to influential executives and extensively invest in relationship-development activities such as social events, vacation homes, and highly experiential outings.
- *Private Equity, Wealthy Individuals, or Merger and Acquisition Advisers.* This includes those in the business of finance. If they don't have the capital themselves, they know people who have access to it. They would also make strong choices for your board of directors or advisers.

Here are two examples of my own relevant contacts and reciprocal relationships:

- *National Speaker's Association and Council of Peers Award for Excellence (CPAE) members*—These are hall of fame international speakers and often masters of thought-provoking content and unparalleled stage presence. Their oratory skills are unmatched and they are able to captivate, inspire, and transform. This is a group from which I can learn a great deal and continue to develop my craft in this arena.

- *HSM World Business Forum*—Once a year at the famed Radio City Music Hall, a high-profile group of legendary leaders, remarkable thinkers, and exceptional achievers—those like Jack Welch, Colin Powell, Michael Porter, and John Chambers, to name a few—gather to share their insights on change, innovation, strategy, and opportunities in emerging multinationals. These are people with whom I aspire to share a stage.

It is not critical that you know exactly who a pivotal contact is, as long as you are able to describe them. (For example, CPAE members are typically in the top 1 percent of their profession.) Do your homework on these people and search for commonalities, opportunities to engage, and most important, avenues in which you can become an asset to them.

Relationship-Centric Best Practice: Relevant Contacts and Reciprocity

Once you have identified the "buckets," focus on individual contacts and how they relate to your goals. Identify 10 such individuals. Print them as a simple list on one page with your goal and contact information, and give it to the most valuable relationships you develop. This approach will allow you to leverage one of the most fundamental characteristics of value-based relationships—that of reciprocity.

Relationship-Centric Best Practice:
Pivotal Contacts and Philanthropic Causes

Pivotal contacts who have achieved material success in life are often attracted to two fundamental opportunities providing your best path to reach them:

- Many are deeply passionate about a philanthropic cause. Often, these causes are related to a personal experience such as a child with autism, a passing parent with Alzheimer's, or the great results they have experienced firsthand, thanks to the American Cancer Society or American Red Cross. Put yourself in a position to quantifiably contribute to their passion.

  Stuart Johnson, a friend and respected corporate attorney at Powell Goldstein, LLP, here in Atlanta, is not only a fellow Eagle Scout, but also extremely passionate about the scouting mission. Beyond his professional success and respected circle of friends and admirers, Stuart deeply believes in making a very real difference as an active adviser in the scouting organization.

  Harry Volande, EVP and CFO of Siemens Energy and Automation, annually leads the Light the Night Walk for the Leukemia and Lymphoma Society. In 2007, they raised $1.4 million. When little Chloe Baker, a leukemia survivor, is around Harry, you feel his compassion as evidenced by his ear-to-ear grin in the presence of this beautiful little girl and her sheer resiliency.

- Another avenue of opportunity is to invite pivotal contacts to highly experiential events. It is one thing to own a Porsche. But it is an entirely different experience to drive one at 160 MPH around Road Atlanta. Create exclusive and memorable experiences for key pivotal contacts you aspire to meet.

For example, our good friends John and Pam Moye in Denver own a beautiful villa in Tuscany. What a great opportunity to invite close friends to experience the tranquil beauty of the Italian countryside in this day and age of hustle and bustle in our daily lives. Jim and Elizabeth Munson regularly attend 20-plus black tie events per year, often inviting those they deem most interesting to a number of unique and sought-after gatherings.

Pivotal Contact Prioritized Matrix of Relationship Investments

If you genuinely believe that pivotal contacts can in fact accelerate your ability to achieve key goals and objectives, it is not difficult to see that prioritizing those relationship investments will become a fundamental challenge. On any given day, you can pursue a plethora of pivotal contacts, all of which could be great assets. But how do you know which ones? A traditional analysis model looks in the rearview mirror to make forward projections. But with changing goals and objectives and constant shifts in the position and business stature of those pivotal contacts, this prioritization is a classic scenario for a perfect storm and certainly a moving target.

An intelligent approach to this prioritization is a simple, yet practical, matrix based on depth, relevancy, spectrum of access, required investment effort, and anticipated return on impact. Let's look at each.

Breadth and Depth

Consider the individual's breadth and depth in your target industry, geography, and functional expertise. How much of a mover and shaker is this person? In the matrix in Figure 6.2, the left-hand side characterizes *specialists*. The more you shift to the right,

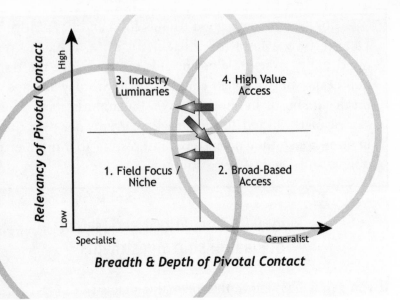

FIGURE 6.2 Pivotal Contacts Prioritized Matrix.

the more *generalist* the characterization becomes. *Specialists* are niche players who are narrow in their focus (example: a neurologist). *Generalists* are the jack of all trades, the generic connectors who know a lot of people and shake a lot of hands (example: politicians). Both groups know a lot of people, but the neurologist is typically very focused on his or her chosen field and will primarily have contacts within that field. Conversely, a politician can talk about anything with anybody. Breadth and depth contributes to how pivotal a contact truly is.

Relevancy

How relevant is the individual to your immediate and quantifiable set of goals and objectives? Though a given person may be able to introduce you to a U.S. senator, this connection doesn't solve your immediate revenue challenges.

On the Y-axis of the graph, there is a scale from low to high relevancy to your immediate goals and objectives. This matrix allows you to identify, and more importantly, prioritize, the four types of pivotal contacts that are directly relevant to your specific goals, strategies, objectives, and tactics.

- *High Value (4)*—These are generalists with a high degree of relevancy.
- *Luminaries (3)*—These are specialists that are highly relevant to your goals, strategies, objectives, and tactics. They are not only highly visible, but should be a particular focal point of your efforts.
- *Broad-based (2)*—These are generalists who know a lot of people or have broad-based access to a lot of people, many of whom are completely irrelevant to your efforts.
- *Niche (1)*—Niche pivotal contacts are specialists, and as such, experts in their respective fields, but they have a low relevancy to your desired relationship-centric outcome. Although it is good to know these individuals, you will seldom see an immediate impact on their relationship investments.

We recommend prioritizing your pivotal contacts according to the above matrix by High Value, Luminaries, Broad-based, and Niche (4–3–2–1).

Spectrum of Access

This is often a question of business stature and broad-based reach. Some people can get you in to see a mayor, while others have access to the president. An individual's spectrum of access expands from local to regional to national to global. (See Figure 6.3.)

This does not refer to a solitary incident or a point in time. We're not talking about you scalping a ticket for me once in the nosebleed section of a global economic forum, but instead identifying who has that consistent, genuine level of access.

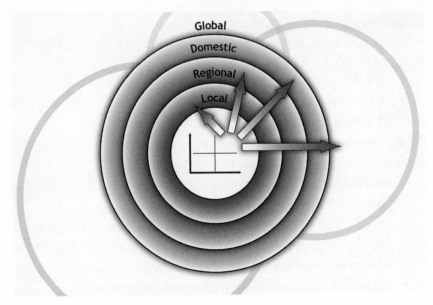

FIGURE 6.3   Spectrum of Access Radar.

Required Investment Effort

What kind of investment of time and effort would it take to get to someone who has access to the president? During a recent political fundraiser at the home of a wealthy executive, it became very clear very quickly that only those with access to long-time party supporters had been extended an invitation. Generous contributors sat at the candidate's dinner table while the rest of the attendees were fanned out according to their spectrum of access radar.

It requires one level of investment to create the kind of access that gets you into a political fundraiser, but it requires a whole different level of investment to get invited to the Oval Office. Think about it: What would it take for you to get to the CEO of GM, for example? What kind of relationships would you need to gain that level of access to those kinds of circles?

Pivotal contacts are instrumental to your personal and professional success. By prioritizing your focus, efforts, and relationship investments, you can create and capitalize on accelerated paths for access to and opportunities with these highly influential individuals. In the next chapter, I discuss how to begin by fully making use of your existing portfolio of relationships—your *Relationship Bank*.

7

Relationship Bank for Strategy Execution

The desired outcomes of any strategic initiative—delighted customers, a motivated and prepared workforce, efficient and effective processes, and, of course, satisfied shareholders— are directly related to how well an organization can link personal actions to its strategic direction. Contrary to popular belief, this takes more than just people. It takes the *relationships* of those change agents to really make things happen.

In this chapter, I discuss the three critical components of an individual, team, or organization's Relationship Bank: diversity, quality, and the required investment efforts.

No Shortage of Strategy Formulation

Strategy formulation is not in short supply. Marty Gupta of CAP Consulting Group often refers to the 10 Schools of Strategy from *Strategy Safari* by Henry Mentzberg. (See Figure 7.1.) They include:

1. *Design*—(1957-plus) where strategy formulation is a deliberate process of conception owned by the CEO, kept simple and easy to communicate, where structure follows strategy with SWOT analysis as its centerpiece tool. Often used for organizations coming out of a period of change into operating stability, where information is available and with organizations that can implement a central strategy.

2. *Planning*—(1965-plus) through a formal process, formal training, and formal analysis involving lots of numbers by the CEO and the staff. Strategies are often full blown with objectives, budgets, programs, and operating plans. It is often very controlling and include scenario planning and strategic control tools. Often used for stable, predictable, and controllable situations.

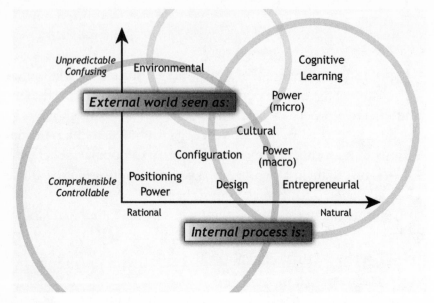

FIGURE 7.1 10 Schools of Strategy.

3. *Positioning*—(1980-plus) focused on an analytical process, it is one of the most common approaches as it is highly analytical with market growth and share matrix, an experience curve, Michael Porter's five-force analysis, and value-chain analysis as its common tools. Porter's strategies often dive into cost leadership, differentiation, and focus of the business. Often used for predictive, established, and stable situations.

4. *Entrepreneurial*—one of a visionary process and leadership where strategy is rooted in the experience and intuition of the leader. The strategy is based on searching for new growth-oriented market opportunities and dramatic leaps forward in the face of uncertainty in a malleable organization. Often used in controllable, comprehensive, situations.

5. *Cognitive*—heavily involved in the mental process with analogies, metaphors, and models. Mapping becomes valuable

where strategies emerge as perspectives. Tools include Myers-Briggs. Often used in unpredictable and uncertain situations.

6. *Learning*—derived through an emergent process where strategy is evolutionary and emergent and as such can't be controlled. Focus is on learning and knowledge creation with systems thinking, core competencies, strategic intent, and knowledge management as useful tools. Often used for unpredictable and uncertain situations.

7. *Power*—relies on negotiation where strategy is shaped by power and politics. Micro power sees strategy formation as the result of persuasion, bargaining, and perhaps confrontation among parochial interests and shifting coalitions, with none dominating over any significant period of time. Macro power uses alliances and social networks inside and outside the organization to control or cooperate. Micro power works in uncertain situations while macro power requires more stability.

8. *Cultural*—formation as a collective process of social interactions. The focus is on corporate culture, values, beliefs, and behaviors and uses tools such as socialization, indoctrination, and ideology to perpetuate existing strategy.

9. *Environmental*—often a reactive process with strategy as ecological model where the environment is the central factor. The organization must respond to these forces or be selected out, where the environment is read and adapted to. Often used in highly uncertain situations.

10. *Configuration*—one of a transformation process focused on strategic change or change management. Life cycle analogy with the recognition of the need for transformation without destroying the organization. Tools included incremental change programs, reengineering and top-down transformation.

Frustrations of Strategy Execution

The breakdown of a great many approaches to delivering strategic outcomes—which are fundamentally designed to satisfy shareholders, delighted customers, and create efficient and effective processes and build a motivated and prepared workforce—is a lack of strategy execution.

Much of this Strategy Execution Pyramid begins with an organization's mission (why we exist), its core values and beliefs (what is important to us), its vision (what we want to be), and its strategy (our game plan to get us there). (See Figure 7.2.)

I call this nothing more than *wall art*. Have you ever seen these often vague and nebulous statements not only spouted out, but actually worshipped and accepted as the end-all and be-all to the company's overall success? Many companies go as far as framing these and glorifying them in their corporate hallways, yet ask three individuals in different geographies or functional silos of the company and they will give you three very different answers on where the organization is headed.

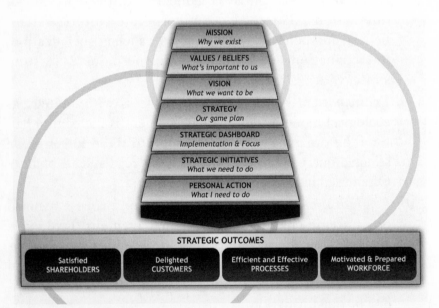

FIGURE 7.2 Strategy Execution Pyramid.

Can you imagine driving a car without a dashboard? Most would agree that this would be ludicrous, yet many organizations don't operate in real time, based on input from a *strategic dashboard*. Not only should the status of current strategic implementations help you gauge your progress, determine whether you are on the right track, and close the gap between your current and future state, but it should also help your organization better focus its valuable resources such as limited capital and critical relationships.

What are some of the strategic initiatives outlining what we need to do and—even if we *can*—who is responsible for asking whether or not we *should* do certain things? Specific actions we need to take are seldom ever tied to corporate mandated strategic initiatives, nor is the dashboard we discussed earlier used to track their progress.

For some reason—perhaps fear of the global war on talent—we continue to lower the bar and aim to accept less. We reward tenure over performance and as such, reject the notion of holding the entire organization, specific teams, and certain individuals accountable for their lack of willingness, ability, and sheer will and determination to make things happen.

Figure 7.3 highlights *four common fundamental barriers to strategy execution:* division, management, people, and resources. Let's examine each one closely.

Division Barrier—In our research, we have found that only 5 percent of the workforce really understands the company's strategy. Down in the mailroom, where the simple execution of the strategy is critical, there is often the biggest disconnect between everyday actions and broader strategic initiatives. This ultimately reduces efficiency and effectiveness and halts the communication of a common vision.

Management Barrier—Some 85 percent of executive teams spend less than one hour a month discussing their strategic options.

People Barrier—Only 25 percent of managers have incentives linked to strategy. If you want to know someone's

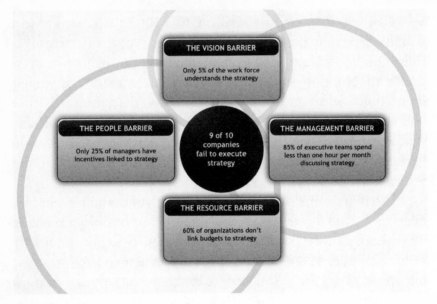

FIGURE 7.3   Barriers to Execution.

motivation, follow the money. Which strategy execution-centric (read: performance-based) moves their needles and get their attention to execute? This applies to a broad-based audience previously made comfortable by the welfare state of a presumed paycheck.

Resource Barrier—Some 60 percent of organizations don't link their budgets to strategy. Is there any real surprise that 9 out of 10 companies fail to execute on their strategy?

Relationship Bank as a Key Enabler

So, if these barriers are the problems, what is the solution? We believe change agents or catalysts at their fundamental core are relationship-centric. Don't confuse vibration with forward motion. Nothing will ever trump performance and as such, if you choose to deliver less than what the market expects, you will ultimately lose. Conversely, with execution, performance, and results, an organization's change agents can leverage their Relationship Banks to institutionalize the desired changes.

Most people do a terrible job of leveraging their existing relationships. You have already spent years, if not decades, working with key individuals you already know and who already know and trust you, yet you haven't touched base with them in years. Did those relationships really fade or did they simply grow cobwebs and rust?

Your portfolio of relationships is your most valuable asset. Within that portfolio, three characteristics are of extreme importance: diversity, quality, and quantity. Look at the people you already know and let's categorize them in several areas.

- *Relevance*—See Relationship Quality Pyramid later in this section.
- *Geographic*—Atlanta, Northeast, West Coast, Europe
- *Function*—Recruiter, Legal, Finance, VC
- *Stature*—Higher than you, lower, the same
- *Organization*—American Management Association, Rotary, PTA
- *Other (nonwork related)*—Friends, neighbors, nonprofits, church
- *Time Known*—less than one year, one to three years, three to five years, 5 to 10 years, 10-plus years
- *Maintain Effort*—How much time do you spend maintaining this relationship?—(1 hour a month, two to three hours a month, one hour a week, two to three hours a week)
- *Interaction Frequency*—Never, sometimes, often, frequently, very frequently

Unless you can categorize your portfolio of relationships into distinct groups, it will be difficult to gauge any meaningful or comparable quality scale. Furthermore, to create impactful connections, you must effectively align your current relationships with the ones you want and need.

Similar to pivotal contacts, in which the decision role and level of access are critical attributes, three critical components within your Relationship Bank can help you effectively prioritize the breadth and depth of your relationships today. In short, they should help you answer—Do you have *contacts* or do you have *relationships*?

They are:

- Your Relationship Value Pyramid
- Their level of influence
- Invested time and effort you are proactively making in each

Now we'll take a closer look at each relationship

Relationship Value Pyramid

Let's begin with the depth and relevancy of your current relationships. For years, I have searched for a process to systematically distinguish the broad-based business stature of my existing relationships. Unable to find one, we created the *Relationship Value Pyramid*. (See Figure 7.4.)

Before we look at each of the levels, it is important to point out that this graphic does not imply that some people are more valuable than others—everyone has value. Instead, the purpose here is to focus on the relevancy of each person in this chapter of your professional life, the nature of your current relationship, and the frequency in which you are likely to interact.

Situation

Your interaction with these people is occasional, your relationship very friendly and collegial. You interact with them because you need to for a particular project, or in a specific department

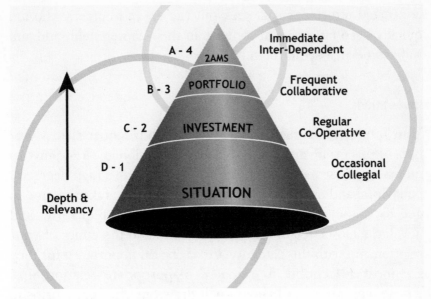

FIGURE 7.4 Relationship Value Pyramid.

or event-based situation. If that situation were to change, more than likely so would the nature of your interaction and relationship. Think of past neighbors, colleagues, project teams with outside consultants, or an industry association you no longer actively participate in.

When possible, automate your outreach to this you-never-know group. Well over 27,000 opt-in subscribers who may have heard me speak at a conference or attended one of our training sessions receives our sought-after monthly newsletter. They may not think of Relationship Economics to solve a critical business challenge today, but you never know when a CEO will read the article in a recent edition—*Will you get a Second Life in the New Year?*—and call us to inquire about our social networking strategy road map. Similarly, you can't afford to ignore what we believe is 50 percent of an individual's portfolio of relationships because you really never know when these dynamic roles, market opportunities, and event-driven situations will become an asset to your efforts. Yet this is also too broad of an audience for any concerted effort. Instead, seek out the up-and-comers who are quickly becoming pivotal contacts in their chosen fields and aim to become an asset to them.

Investment

Your interaction is regular, your relationship cooperative. Members of this group are a lot like you. As mentioned earlier, investments are those individuals with which you have a high degree of behavioral and psychological profile similarities. Take the time to get to know them better, collaborate more frequently, and develop a closer relationship. The tactics and the ethics of your relationship with this category are of critical importance for they are most susceptible to *perceived* inappropriate relationships. Those who are most like you will draw out cries of favoritism, nepotism, and "foul play."

You may have a strong relationship with this group and cooperate with them on key initiatives, but they may or may not be of the highest value to your relevant goals and objectives. Remember that the aim is to heavily invest in those who can influence the achievement of your goals or create access to those who can directly help. This group should ideally make up 25 percent of your portfolio of relationships.

Portfolio

These are the go-to people in your portfolio of relationships. They are subject matter, geographic, or functional experts. Your interactions are frequent and your relationship is very collaborative. The relationship is one of equal stature and perceived value-add. If value is diminished in one scenario, it is easily replenished in another.

These are high-value targets. To build deeper relationships, focus on close family ties and interactions, or nonwork-related interactions over an extended period of time. This group should ideally compose 15 percent of your portfolio of relationships.

2 A.M.S

Not only will this group not get upset if you call them at 2 A.M., they will come and bail you out of jail! Your access to them is immediate and you have a very interdependent relationship.

These are former bosses, mentors, coaches, and other select people with a very real vested interest in your well-being and success. These people are the real gems in your portfolio of relationships. Protect them at all costs, take care of them, never let them down, and constantly aim to remain an asset to them. These are mentors who can provide pearls of wisdom and valuable access to pivotal contacts most relevant to your goals. They know you very well, so leverage their insights as sounding boards and gauge your personal and professional strengths and weaknesses from their candor. Never embarrass them or even hint to the outside world any weaknesses or shortcomings they may possess.

This group should be your lifelong mission in developing relationships and should make up the remaining 10 percent of your relationship portfolio. It has been our experience that senior executives who heavily guard their most intimate relationships have single digit 2 A.M.s—a very select few whom they have known for years. They have vacationed together, are childhood friends, college roommates, or have met through a special circumstance. To be clear—these 2 A.M.s are *professional* relationships beyond your close personal friends and family members.

Level of Influence

The second critical attribute in your Relationship Bank is the level of influence of your key members. Their level of influence is critical because of the notion of credibility by association. If they are respected, trusted, and held in high regard, when you become an asset to them, will that level of influence be an asset to you in return?

Six levels are identified in Figure 7.5, ranging from a very high level of influence to none and "don't know." (Which begs

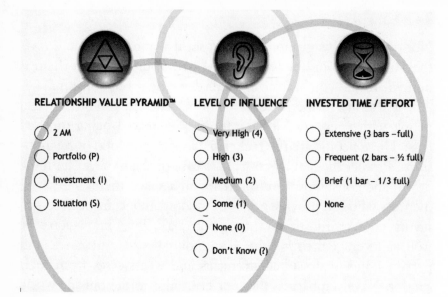

RELATIONSHIP VALUE PYRAMID™	LEVEL OF INFLUENCE	INVESTED TIME / EFFORT
2 AM	Very High (4)	Extensive (3 bars –full)
Portfolio (P)	High (3)	Frequent (2 bars – ½ full)
Investment (I)	Medium (2)	Brief (1 bar – 1/3 full)
Situation (S)	Some (1)	None
	None (0)	
	Don't Know (?)	

FIGURE 7.5   Relationship Bank Attributes.

the question, How can you tell if someone has a high level of influence?)

Look around. Listen intently. Observe. Are there ideas being implemented? How are they thought about or spoken of in this contact's absence? Would an unscientific survey of 5 to 10 colleagues provide any insights? Are they able to get critical functions or tasks accomplished often without authority over others? Are they clearly and consistently in the inner circle of what's happening versus asking what just happened?

Time and Effort Invested

The last attribute in this area is the time and effort you have invested with this individual in your Relationship Bank. Keeping in mind a holistic perspective, would you consider your investments *extensive, frequent, brief,* or *none?* To truly realize the full potential of any relationship, you must invest the time and effort to really get to know them and to truly understand that which they hold dear. You have to become savvy in the realm of their currency.

Diversity, Quality, and Required Investment Efforts

To effectively leverage the quality scale, you should begin by categorizing your existing relationships according to this pyramid. Twice a year, print out your entire contact database (from your Outlook, Act, Palm, BlackBerry, and so forth). Preventive maintenance of your most valuable relationships will reduce the likelihood of failure of future Relationship Currency exchanges when needed the most. Go through each individual contact and ask yourself the following questions:

- When did I last speak to or see him?
- Is she still at the same company, location, and function?
- Is this a person in whom I have previously invested with no return on that relationship investment or is it someone whom I have neglected and need to prioritize in the next six months?
- Is this person still relevant to my goals and objectives or someone whom, similar to my closet, I have neglected to clean out?

Please note that I am not advocating discarding people simply because they are no longer of value to you! Instead, I am suggesting that we are all busy and pressed for time. You simply cannot invest your finite resources (time, effort, and capital) on everyone equally. If, in any given day, you could interact with 50 people, for example, how would you prioritize which 50 out of the hundreds, if not thousands, you know? Some would simply say, "The 50 people I have to deal with at any given time." Unfortunately, this is very narrow-minded, because many of those are situational relationships that will change as your circumstances change. All the while, you are neglecting critical members of your Relationship Bank. Although we have addressed the relationships you need, it is also critical to point out the fundamental value in proactively seeking to understand relationships others need with you. Are they transitory or enduring and how can you nurture those relationships accordingly?

Here's a question for you: What was that really important project you were working on in the fall of 2000? Conversely, who was that manager who really invested in you, who cared about your personal and professional development and took you under his wing to make sure you turned out okay? Most people don't recall those critical project deadlines or deals, but they will never forget the key people who have molded their careers, characters, and lasting relationships.

Relationship-Centric Best Practice: Relationship Value Pyramid

Sit down, find a quiet time, and dust the cobwebs off your past relationships. Document all of the different *buckets* where you currently have or previously have had great relationships. Of particular interest are investment, portfolio, and 2 A.M. contacts. We often find that, when dealing with 2 A.M.s, it really doesn't matter how long you have been apart. With many relationships, you can simply pick up where you left off and five minutes into that initial phone call, it will seem like you just saw each other yesterday.

Take an inventory of your relationships. Jog your memory and create a list of people you know in each section. Identify the source of the contact, individual members, and their relationship relevancy. Start with your most immediate interactions—let's call them the *Today Chapter* of your life:

- Current colleagues (people you pass in the hallway every day)
- Industry and civic associations
- Personal friends/neighbors/poker night
- Sports leagues/golf clubs/kids' involvement
- Faith-based acquaintances
- Other

Now for the *Yesterday Chapter:*

- Most recent job (colleagues, clients, suppliers)
- Former industry associations
- Last neighborhood/civic organization/nonprofit board
- Other

Education:
- Undergraduate/grad school/law school/medical school alumni
- Executive education program
- Study abroad
- Other

Special Circumstances:
- Travel/vacation/Peace Corp
- Tragedy/disaster (9/11, Katrina relief)
- Awards/achievements (President's Club, Olympic Torch relay)

Your Past:
- Childhood friends/neighbors
- Parents' friends/colleagues
- Other

We have become such a transient society that many of us lose touch with over 90 percent of the people we work with when we change jobs or move to another city. We get bogged down with the day-to-day grunt of our new roles and simply forget the people with whom we spent hours, if not days, weeks, and months on projects, those whom we really appreciated getting to know.

The good news is that old friends don't go away—they simply fade. Google them. Call someone else you know who may have stayed in touch with that person. Find them and reconnect, reengage, and create a reason to see each other again whether they are on the next street, in the next town, or clear across the country.

To summarize this section on the importance of your Relationship Bank, keep in mind the following topics and focus on achieving:

Categorize your current relationships. Who are the influential people you already know? How long have you known them? How much time and effort do you invest to nurture those relationships? Are you leveraging the most quantifiable value from each? You can't improve what you can't measure. Begin by categorizing the relationships you already have. Don't forget—relevancy and diversity are the two most valuable assets in your Relationship Bank.

Build and nurture your key relationships. Once you have categorized your existing relationships, you can set out a course to nurture and leverage the crucial ones in which you've deemed it appropriate to invest. What did you bring to the table for your most valuable relationships? Expand your bank by getting involved in diverse projects, teams, and organizations. Openly share your goals and objectives and solicit best practices from those you trust and respect. Share best practices as often as possible.

Make bank account enhancements. Like the clothes in your closet, do an inventory of your Relationship Bank every year.

Prioritize those who have invested in your success and de-prioritize those in whom you have invested but didn't see a return on your relationship investment. Proactively seek out those of higher stature, subject matter expertise, or different focus.

So far, we have covered Relationship-Centric Goals, which are business goals that will require a relationship with others to achieve; pivotal Contacts as individuals instrumental to your personal and professional success; and key metrics around your existing Relationship Bank. A logical question at this point would be to then ask, "How do I connect the people I know to the ones I need to get to know better in a nonthreatening value-based approach?" Glad you asked. Read on.

8

Relationship Currency
for Adaptive Innovation

It has been said that it is less expensive to innovate than it is to advertise. Yet most organizations are satisfied with incrementalism—a me-too way of doing things *better*. In contrast, true innovation is about doing things *differently*. It focuses on the investment of an organization's most valuable asset—its portfolio of relationships—to capture and leverage best practices across the organization and across the globe. In this chapter, I define *Relationship Currency*: what it is, how it really works, and how to leverage it most effectively toward adaptive innovation.

Exchanging Relationship Currency

Exchanging Relationship Currency is how you bridge the gap between the trusted relationships you currently have with the influential relationships you need. In its most simple definition, Relationship Currency is a gift of time, talent, knowledge, or an influential relationship that is exchanged between individuals with the intent of adding quantifiable value. As you rekindle old relationships or seed new ones, your key goal should always be to uncover what is important to each of them so that you can make an appropriate *deposit* of Relationship Currency. Here are some simple methods.

Become More Interesting

Did you know that only an estimated 27 percent of all Americans have a valid passport? Travel, whether domestically or abroad, is a perfect opportunity to expand your horizons, provide unique perspectives on very different social styles, and in the process, hopefully provide you with a new outlook not only on how we as U.S. citizens view the world, but also how the rest of the world views us. Developing an interest in the performing arts or a passion for a philanthropic cause can also expose you to opportunities that provide unique value-add to a variety of personal and professional interactions.

I recently had the opportunity to participate in the new member program trip to Hong Kong, Beijing, Shanghai, and Xi'an with the Society of International Business Fellows (SIBF). Not only did we enjoy breathtaking views from the InterContinental Hong Kong hotel, Peninsula Palace Beijing, and the Four Seasons Hotel Shanghai, but we also attended panel discussions with:

- Cynthia Watson, chairwoman of the Department of Security Studies at the National War College
- Sameena Ahmad, Asia business and finance correspondent, the *Economist*
- Eden Woon, CEO, Hong Kong General Chamber of Commerce
- Jonathan Anderson, managing director, Asia-Pacific Economics, UBS Investment Bank
- Shai Oster, correspondent, *Wall Street Journal*, Asia
- Jamie Florcruz, Beijing Bureau Chief, CNN
- Kenneth Jarrett, U.S. consul general, Shanghai

I had the chance to experience a very unique and firsthand perspective on the challenges and opportunities in China alongside a very talented group of senior executives, many of whom I hope will become lifelong friends. That experience has helped me engage some of my most valuable relationships with insightful comments and unique perspectives.

While I was there, the cultural influences I experienced—such as a private concert by the Peking Opera at the exclusive China Club, Beijing, and tour of the Forbidden City (and not to mention rappelling off the Great Wall, where Genghis Kahn broke through many centuries ago)—enlightened and humbled me to the vast amount of opportunities available to expand one's sheer capacity to grow personally and professionally.

Build a Personal Brand

What is that brand of clothing with the famous checkmark? How about the shop around the corner with the $10 cup of coffee? How about the red can of soda that we all order by name? As previously mentioned, companies spend billions of dollars annually to enhance their brand equity.

Regardless of your profession, when others engage you, buy from you, work with you, or trust and invest in you, they are in essence buying three things: your product or service, the perception of the company behind that product or service, and the brand called *you*. This is not unlike corporate brand equity. Your personal brand equity also differentiates you from competing mind share and wallet share among a sea of sameness.

Only by elevating yourself above this noise and (hopefully) creating personal brand attributes such as competence, intellect, solid judgment, integrity, and dependability will you be selected for critical projects and true leadership roles, and viewed as one who will create access to strategic relationships.

Become Known for Content

I would submit that it is better to be known for content than it is to simply be known. When I say *Good to Great, Execution, In Search of Excellence, Blue Ocean Strategy, The 7 Habits of Highly Effective People, Blink,* and *Freakonomics,* what comes to the minds of many are the world-renowned authors behind these well-known works.

When you are known for content, you are sought after. You are asked to speak, moderate panels, and share your experiences, insights, and perspectives. Take a trade show, for example:

You can *exhibit* there, set up a booth and pass out marketing materials; you can *attend* the show and sit through content sessions; or you can *speak* or moderate a panel at the event. Which do you believe would have the greatest impact? Each has its respective value, but the latter often leaves a much more meaningful and lasting impression. So, how do you get invited to speak? What value-add do you contribute to the event? What forward-looking or contrarian perspective can you bring? That is your highly valuable and unique content.

Content takes research, packaging, and marketing in the form of white papers, published articles, columns, and books. Content is constantly in demand. Yet I am mesmerized by the sheer number of CEOs I continue to meet—many true subject matter experts in their respective fields—who have never written or submitted their unique perspectives on topics that they are visually very passionate about. What they don't realize is that, by being perceived as thought leaders in their fields, they would create an unparalleled market pull for their respective organizations.

Here are some examples of how Relationship Currency works and the relevant deposits you can make.

- While talking to a colleague who was recently transferred to your division, he notices something from your college on the wall and mentions that his son is interested in applying to that same school. As an alumnus, is there something you can do to assist your colleague? Can you make a call to someone in admissions or provide a campus tour? By the way, no one has perfected the campus tour experience quite like Nido Qubein, president of High Point University in High Point, North Carolina. His highly student-centric approach provides every student an opportunity for an extraordinary education in a fun environment with caring people.
- Over coffee with a client, she mentions how busy she has been working on a charity silent auction and how she desperately needs unique donations. Offer to call a neighbor

who is a strong sponsor of Cirque du Soleil and entice her to become likewise passionate in the campaign.

- You read in the paper that an old friend has been promoted to a new VP position. Call to congratulate him, and offer to introduce him to a senior executive at your company to explore possible synergies.

It is critical to remember that what people do for a living is not who they are. If you don't give people a chance to get to know you, how do you expect them to trust you? Someone protested recently, "But trust comes with time and experience in dealing with that person. Aren't you really looking for faith?" Well said! People want to believe that you are credible *today* and believe in you *tomorrow* as you begin to deliver some of the value you promised *yesterday*!

Get to Know People—Ask Better Questions

If you are determined to go beyond the superficial and really begin to get to know others, you must start by asking better questions. Beyond the obvious, *"How have you been? How was your weekend?"* Try:

- If you were going to create a new role here, what would it be and why?
- What are you passionate about when you're not at the office?
- What are the top three goals you want to achieve this year?
- How are you measured?

Only by changing your behavior to stop winging it and becoming more disciplined and intentional with your questions will you really get to the core of who your colleagues really *are* versus simply what they *do*.

Get People out of Their Offices

Most offices have stiff chairs. Most coffee shops have comfortable couches. Get people out of their office and engage them—really engage them—over a cup of coffee. If you don't like coffee, drink tea. If you don't like tea, drink water. If you have a corporate cafeteria, take them there. It's never about the meal. It's about the opportunity to engage, interact, and getting to know each other better outside the day-to-day grind.

You Can't Clone Yourself, but You Can Clone Time

Most people get a perplexed look on their face when I say this, but think about it: If you are meeting someone for a 10 A.M. cup of coffee (and if it's appropriate), why not invite someone at 9:30, visit with them, and overlap the two visits by 15 to 30 minutes so you can introduce the two people you are visiting with to each other? This gives them a chance to meet and extend their own portfolio of relationships. Just remember that no one likes surprises, so run the idea by both parties beforehand. Also make sure to discuss sensitive, personal, and no other party-relevant topics on your individual times.

Start by Making a Deposit!

Your Relationship Currency exists in an account that is very similar to your checking account, and you can't write a check from an account in which you have no money. You can't make a withdrawal without making a deposit first. You also can't deposit $100 and attempt to withdraw $1,000. These principles are equally consistent in your business relationships. We have all experienced far greater ease in asking for a withdrawal if you have previously made the necessary deposits.

It is absolutely mind boggling to me how many people will ask for a favor when they haven't earned the right to do so. I am not advocating that you keep score. When I meet someone, I'm not gauging whether we can do business together or not—I'm looking to understand whether this person gets, appreciates, and leverages the real value of relationships. Reciprocity is a natural and unmistakable law in relationships. Maybe not today, tomorrow, next week, next month, or next year, but those who truly understand the dynamics of the *favor economy* will find a way to eventually reciprocate.

Relationship-Centric Best Practice: Relationship Currency Deposits

To summarize Relationship Currency deposits and discover how to transform relationship creation into relationship capitalization, keep in mind the following simple yet critical precepts.

Reciprocate First. If you begin by really getting to know and truly investing in everyday contacts with meaningful Relationship Currency deposits, the world becomes your ATM.

Establish value-Based Relationships. Aim to deliver value in every interaction. By focusing on that which is of particular value to others, you can sharpen your unique value-add. When you introduce two people to each other and they benefit from that introduction, you have made deposits in *two* accounts.

Build a Personal Brand. In a sea of sameness, being interesting, being known for content, and building a personal brand will differentiate you from the others. By becoming more interesting, you add value to each interaction. Content is by far more valuable than self-promotion. Personal branding can exponentially extend your reach. Research it, package it, market it, and perfect it. People are buying *you*!

Return on Involvement. Pick the organizations in which you choose to invest—whether professional, civic, or

(continued)

Relationship-Centric Best Practice:
Relationship Currency Deposits (Continued)

---

community—carefully. Get engaged or get involved by taking on the most visible roles in areas such as membership, marketing, or programs.

30-60-90–Day Personal Relationship Plan

Only a fundamental change in your behavior will create a lasting impact on your relationship development success. To adopt even some of these ideas to the extent that you are comfortable will help you make many of these best practices yours.

1. *Make a real commitment to start pervasively integrating relationships in your everyday interactions.* Relationship development is not a spectator sport. Attend a function from the sideline and you'll grossly miss the opportunity to meet those critical individuals who can dramatically improve your situation. Start by inviting a colleague to an industry function where you already feel comfortable with your surroundings.

2. *Set quantifiable goals.* Remember: Most New Year's resolutions fail because they don't include a quantifiable way to measure one's progress. Build a 30-60-90–day plan with quantifiable goals, objectives, and action items. Prioritize them into three categories: *Serious* (if you don't do it now, it will hurt you), *Urgent* (if you don't get to it, it will become serious and hurt you) and *Growth* (fire prevention and opportunities for scale).

3. *There is no magic bullet when it comes to building and nurturing lasting relationships.* And when you make mistakes or unintentionally ruin a relationship, there is no pause or restart button. Relationship building is not speed dating; it takes time, effort, and investments. Many are either unwilling or unable

to take this journey. If you're unwilling, neither I nor anyone else can help you. If you're unable, we can address that with coaching, training, mentoring, and supporting technology. You simply have to decide if this aspect of your personal and professional development is important enough to make the necessary investments to do it right and do it well.

4. *There are absolute and very real tradeoffs in the process.* I have two young children and it is always a heartbreaking choice to A) attend another networking function or B) go home to my beautiful wife and kids whom I miss throughout the day, and spend time that I won't get back. There is no easy answer and as hard as many try, real balance is very difficult to obtain. The opportunity cost forces me to do my homework before attending any event. Ideally, I'll have a good idea of the speaker's bio, the nature of their content, and the interests of the audience. If one of these three is not aligned with my personal or professional goals, I don't go. I have elevated my efforts from simply activity-based networking to value-based relationship development in the organizations I belong to, events I attend, and travel commitments I make.

Understanding and beginning to exchange Relationship Currency is the critical first step in your Relationship Economics transformation process. The more you use these techniques, the more confident your mindset, the sharper your toolset, and the clearer and crisper your individual road map will become. Make the commitment to invest the time, effort, and resources in the next 30–60–90 days to make a real change in how you build, nurture, and leverage key relationships toward your personal and professional success.

Less Expensive to Innovate than to Advertise

An organization's most valuable asset is its portfolio of relationships. How they invest in those relationships to capture and leverage best practices across the organization determines how successfully they will be able to reach true innovation.

Relationship-Centric Best Practice: 30-60-90–Day Personal Plan

Over the next 30 days:

- Clean, centralize, update, and value pyramid your current Relationship Bank. Take the time to go through and assign categories, think about how much time you have or need to invest in each, and if they're not relevant, export these contacts into a separate spreadsheet, apart from your active, day-to-day list.
- Identify your top three goals for the next 12 months— inventory your Relationship Currency assets.
- Given your goals, identify and begin profiling three Pivotal Contacts and higher business stature relationships you currently have.
- Get to really know those Pivotal Contacts over coffee or a meal.
- Find an opportunity to become an asset to them early and often.

Over the next 60 days:

- Translate your value-add into a recognizable impact.
- Arm your current relationships with ammunition to introduce you to a Pivotal Contact.
- Meet with a minimum of one Pivotal Contact toward achieving a key goal.

Over the next 90 days:

- Build a pipeline of contacts met, source of those contacts, outcomes of each meeting, and any next steps.
- Leverage one contact to extend your reach to as diverse an audience or network as possible.

- Connect a minimum of three individuals you've met with each other.

Remember these three best practices:
1. Build a "mastermind group of partners" who believe in the real value of relationships. Schedule regular meetings and keep each other accountable.
2. Bring your personalized plan to a weekly meeting and build on this foundation.
3. Start small and with easy or comfortable topics. Success builds on success, so start by attending one event per week or aim to meet one to two new people per week.

What qualities are shared by the candy and beverage company Cadbury Schweppes, Indian automaker Tata Motors, Caterpillar, Apple, Adidas, Toyota, and Christian Dior? According to the Booz Allen Hamilton Global Innovation 1000, they are but a few of the world's relationship-centric innovators. By nurturing highly decentralized and knowledge-driven cultures—irrespective of whether you are the earth-moving equipment giant, the nimble conceptualizer of the iPod Nano, or the German purveyor of quality, yet fashion-conscious sportswear—these smart spenders get a higher return on their R&D investments than many of their highly innovative peers.

Although there is seldom a simple relationship between an organization's overall R&D spend and its corporate performance, adaptive innovation consistently leverages strategic relationships to uncover new innovative practices as well as reinforce metrics such as the number and quality of patents controlled.

Take Apple, for example. Do you really believe that Steve Jobs was the first to think of recording audio on a memory stick? On the contrary, for close to a decade, Sony enjoyed enormous success with the Walkman. It was by far one of history's most successful product launches, executions, and extensions of a consumer products company. But it took Steve Jobs, the Apple DNA, and its relentless focus on the customer experience to not only put the Walkman out of business, but introduce a new market maker in the iPod. By understanding the limitations of the Walkman—as compared to the expansive ability to deliver hundreds, if not thousands, of CDs, individual songs, and even more recently, television shows and entire movies—Apple disrupted the value chain between content creation (the artists), content delivery (traditional music industry channels), and the enormous end user of audio and video content.

When you innovate, it is not only critical to engage in a broad-based scanning of the competitors, market and business drivers, but also to extend that scan into the larger environment and collective social intelligence.

Adaptive Innovation

To adapt to one's dynamic market demands, the organization's relationship-centric DNA must focus its innovation investments on a succinct understanding of the customer's needs coupled with strong marketing and investment planning. In adaptive innovation, seven critical metrics can be greatly enhanced through the systematic and disciplined capitalization of intra-company, as well as external strategic relationships.

- Sales Growth
- Gross Margin Percentage
- Gross Profit Growth
- Operating Margin Percentage
- Operating Income Growth
- Total Shareholder Returns
- Market Capitalization Growth

The broad-based identification and leveraging of company-wide expertise in a multitude of functions, developed over a period of time, can create a very sustainable competitive advantage. Adaptive innovation must be fueled by those at the edge of business, often closest to the voice of the customer. Those investments made for longer horizons focus on creating profitable growth.

Relationship Economics @ Work: Steve McGaw at AT&T and Strategic Relationships at Multiple Business Statures

Relationships are especially important when dealing with business partnerships. For example, when AT&T aligned itself with Yahoo to build a reputation with customers as a strong Internet service provider (ISP), relationships played a critical role because they affected the speed at which the company could actually deploy the technology and new service.

"We had to work through issues that were foreign to both parties," said Steve McGaw, SVP, Mobility Supply Chain and Fleet Operations at AT&T. "As companies, we were coming from very different vantage points. The relationships from top to bottom were really critical from the CEO, to the business development people, to the technology people."

Relationships at multiple business stature levels became vital to the deal, McGraw said.

"In our experience, the only partnerships that we have seen work well have included relationships spanning the corporate hierarchy," McGaw said. "It has to be an institutionalized part of the company. That way, as people come and go, they don't take the partnership with them. This kind of communication has to span multiple levels across different organizations within each company so that everyone understands the overall vision and goals of the partnership."

Adaptive innovation also forces the organization to focus on and invest in its most valuable asset—its portfolio of intracompany as well as externally focused relationships. In all of the organizations we have worked with over the years, I have yet to meet a chief best practices officer. So, whose role is it to capture and leverage the pockets of best practices that abound in any organization?

Innovation aims to leapfrog the competition, and to truly shape an entire industry. Adaptive innovation is about doing things *differently*. This approach requires a relationship-centric culture with the courage to fail and learn from those failures. It is not about simply imitating the strategies of others through traditional value add, but shaping one's own destiny.

It is important to note that innovation is a process with multiple enablers, contributors, and positive components. A single ad never works. Advertising often just contributes to the noise. But when you innovate, the market seeks you out.

Relationship-Centric Innovation Value Disruption

Value creation is derived from value chain disruption. If you don't build strategic relationships to disrupt your value chain, someone else will. As such, adaptive innovation can be characterized as a series of logical processes and critical relationships often interdependent on one another. (See Figure 8.1.) These sequential processes are:

Stage 1: *Seeding*—market research and conceptualizing often far fetched ideas

Stage 2: *Prioritization*—selective decision process

Stage 3: *Product Development and Product Road Map*

Stage 4: *Commercialization*—Adapting, bridging, and aligning with those dynamic customer demands

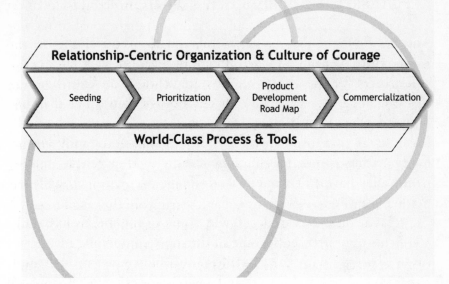

FIGURE 8.1   Adaptive Innovation Value Chain.

These are links in a value chain. And for adaptive innovation to work, these links must be seamlessly integrated and deliver a very high level of consistent performance over time. Relationship-centric DNA focuses heavily on not just the passing of the baton between those critical stages, but being able to do so without knowledge drain. An organization's relationship-centric DNA mitigates market risks and additionally hones an organization's capabilities in project prioritization and subsequently commercialization. This is ideally coupled with a sharp understanding of not only what its customers want, but also what they need.

Adaptive innovation can also greatly benefit from *co-opetition*, where promising ideas are jointly developed and advanced through a consortium. Agility, systematic seeding, and broad-based involvement, including that of the senior leaders (such as Steve Jobs at Apple), in the conceptualization and further refinement of new ideas, are other critical characteristics we've seen in this area.

Portfolio of Relationships as a Differentiating Asset

Another fundamental enabler to relationship-centric innovation is the critical yet often missed notion of location. Face-to-face is still critical for the effective exchange of ideas, and nowhere is this exchange more valuable for technology companies than in Silicon Valley. Paul Romer, professor of the Graduate School of Business at Stanford University, argues that geography absolutely matters and that technology ideas with their genesis in Silicon Valley have an exponential advantage over those brought to market elsewhere.

Have you ever wondered why some of the most successful VC firms that often back some of the most compelling ideas are often obsessed with the 50-mile radius between San Jose and San Francisco? On a quarterly basis, PricewaterhouseCoopers releases its MoneyTree Report, which consistently points to over 25 percent of all venture investments in the United States going to Silicon Valley ideas and ventures.

Strong portfolios of relationships create a highly differentiating asset in this scenario based on two fundamental factors: 1) mover advantage and 2) a noticeably higher return on any of those investments. Some of your best future employees are friends of your current employees. As such, their personal relationships outside of work become a huge determining factor in where they choose to work. And besides, who wouldn't want to work for a rock star of a company like Intel, Apple, or Google (all of which are within a 50-mile radius of San Francisco and San Jose)?

Stephen Adams, an assistant professor of management at the Franklin P. Perdue School of Business at Salisbury University, has studied the rise of Silicon Valley. In his research, he points to the fact that venture capital attracts a lot of ideas, which in turn attract a stronger portfolio of relationships. This genesis of an ecosystem fascinates newcomers who are plugged into existing relationships of seasoned professionals, which allows the right teams to assemble great technology ideas much more quickly than anywhere else in the country. They understand, embrace, and apply adaptive innovation at a much faster rate. They test ideas, fail, learn, reinvent, repurpose, and reintroduce groundbreaking approaches much faster than anywhere else in the world.

That's not to say that Silicon Valley is immune to challenges in establishing and developing sound Relationship Economics practices. The logic of first mover advantage and greater than average returns is also very real along Route 128 in the suburbs around Boston, as well as in many other parts of the world with residents who also know how to commercialize great ideas. There are also fundamental challenges with innovation in places like Silicon Valley. In times of trouble—such as the Internet bubble of 2000 or the housing crisis of 2007 and 2008—the Valley tends to catch a worse cold than the rest of the world. Right after the bust, for example, there was a period of time in which Silicon Valley was seen as overcooked and overdone. The amazing thing is how resilient it has proven to be. Every time there is a failure, it recovers and becomes even more durable.

Fifty years ago, the silicon chip was the growth engine of Silicon Valley. Until the late 1970s, the Japanese memory chip manufacturers stole the show. With the advent of personal computers, data storage software, and more recently the ever-expansive Web, new media, and online commerce, we continue to paint the portfolio of relationships within Silicon Valley as a *wow*. Even with the evolution of technology, personal connections continue to build on the momentum and the ability to consistently adapt models to changing market demands. Deal flow, which is the lifeline of VC firms, is most often driven by the breadth and depth of your portfolio of relationships. More important, value promised and value delivered encompasses the exchange of Relationship Currency.

In all great industries, geographies, organizations, teams, and especially inner circles—beyond the aboveground economy—the fundamental driver linking business innovation to economic prosperity is often the undocumented, unspoken, and underground favor economy. Like cash, Relationship Currency has immediate and extreme liquidity in its value. But it also has a shelf life. People may or may not remember what we did for them 6 or 9 or 12 months ago, but they will remember the value added last week or perhaps last month.

9

Transforming *Us* and *Them* into *We*

In his book, *Winning*, Jack Welch writes about a lack of candor in corporate America. The same is often true with business relationships. We tell people what they want to hear—not what is going to help them become better leaders or even better human beings. We talk about accountability, yet we tolerate mediocrity (at a number of iconic U.S. corporations) and then wonder what the key factors were driving the same company to its eventual demise.

Exemplary professional conduct shouldn't be the exception. Why do we talk about *business ethics* when it should be just *ethics* in general? You either have them or you don't. You seldom meet someone who is incredibly ethical in their personal life, yet laundering money, bribing customers and engaging in corporate espionage against competitors at work. Likewise, quality shouldn't be a *department*—it's a *mindset*. It is an attitude and an organization's deeply rooted belief system that, "We will produce the best product or deliver the best service we can, every time, while we continue to raise the bar for ourselves."

One of the most visible areas in need of candor today is in large-scale change management, sometimes brought on by mergers and acquisitions. A recent Bain study highlighted that less than 30 percent of mergers and acquisitions are deemed successful. A Mercer-Business Week study found that, out of 150 deals valued at $500 million or more, more than half actually *destroyed* shareholder wealth as judged by stock performance. And only one third contributed marginally to shareholder worth.

In this chapter, I cover the fundamental role of change agents and the strategic value of their business relationships with the very organizational departments in need of that change. I discuss the 100-Day Action Plan that every company needs in a large-scale change initiative or merger and acquisitions event and the critical role of strategic business relationships on the influential and the influenced, both inside and outside the organization. In short, how to transform *us* and *them* into *we*.

Strategic Relationships of Key Agents in Navigating Change

A component that is critical to driving everything from process optimization to altering the mindset of the people whom the change will surely affect is the team of employees chartered to help the organization navigate through this often challenging journey. These change agents are leaders in their organizations, free of hierarchical bondage, and are often able to move across a multitude of departments, business units, and divisions in search of simpler processes. They are highly motivated and well-trained employees and absolutely key to implementing better procedures for the maximum output from any organizational investment in limited resources.

Pick this team for their technical skills alone and, in many instances, they will fail. Pick them for their tenure and knowledge of the organization, and they are likely to come up short. Pick a team wholly cut from the same cloth (with similar psychological or behavioral profiles), and they are likely to dismiss those who bring different perspectives in regard to a prioritization of strategic initiatives. They will miss critical components necessary for a successful transformation of the organization. Pick them carelessly and the cost will not be too dissimilar to that of a bad executive hire—at least 10 to 12 times their combined annual salary. And that doesn't take into consideration the corporate reputation and perceived inability of the leadership team to assign a competent, credible, and emotionally intelligent team to lead the very change communicated to be strategic to the organization's future.

Consider, for example, a manufacturing client that assembled a team of change agents to drive its lean-operations initiative. The group reported directly to senior executives and was staffed with a team of young, energetic, fresh thinking new hires—real innovators. Unfortunately, senior leadership failed to recognize the covert and overt pushback by the business units' NIH (*not invented here*) culture and silo mentality.

As a result, operations managers with very real organizational power felt invaded by "a group of kids who simply didn't 'get' how we do things around here." The management team was left with few choices other than to abandon the change initiative after just a few months. The change agents did not focus on fostering strategic relationships—those that could influence the broader mindset and help position their great ideas as, "a fresh set of eyes on a stagnant industry and its complacent workforce." They did not establish themselves as trustworthy in combining their credibility (knowledge of highly efficient and effective processes, combined with empathy) with the value of experience from a highly tenured team. Trust leads to candor; candor leads to prudent risk taking; risk taking leads to innovation.

Our experience with a variety of organizations that have succeeded in crafting and executing real change suggests that it is critical to have strategic and intentional relationship development competencies of a carefully constructed change agent team. Three essential components include:

- *Quantifiable impetus for change and the opportunity cost of status quo*—To understand the essence of *why* we must change, people must believe in the real, financial impact on their lives if they *don't* embark on this journey. Without that understanding, the idea of change itself will seldom strike the necessary chord to move. Another fundamental challenge is that of the status quo, which does not represent alternatives to change, but rather the most destructive option of all—that of simply doing nothing. Unless the opportunity cost of the status quo is likewise presented in real dollars and cents, very few will want to move away from their current comfort zone.

- *Careful recruitment and development of the change agent team*—Clearly articulating the benefits and opportunities team members will receive because of nontraditional career paths, particularly when selecting high performers already well-respected within the company, sends a clear signal that management takes the program seriously. This group must possess the raw analytical power to solve complex business problems as well as highly astute interpersonal skills, including empathy, strong communication skills, perseverance, and creativity in the face of challenge or ambiguity. This is particularly critical when dealing with conflict. They must be constructive and aim to strike a balance between young MBA types and seasoned managers with proven track records within the organization.

- *Close relationship development and nurturing between the change agent team and the influential members of the organizational areas targeted for transformation*—Alan Weiss has often coached me that, "With eighty percent completion of anything—move. The remaining twenty percent seldom matters." By developing a close working relationship with the shop floor, your buy-in rate as a critical success metric for real change increases exponentially.

Encourage open, candid communication that keeps key influential team members actively engaged in the change process and involves them in complex problem-solving sessions. This helps build personal connections to and ownership of the solution. Testing proposed ideas and making iterative modifications creates small wins, which can be transformed into standard tools and processes and can serve as a flywheel of momentum for the rest of the organization. Communication and collaboration serve as an enabler, not just to inciting change, but to leveraging relationships to overcome barriers to lasting impactful change.

Network of Influencers as a Strategic Asset in Change Management

Several years ago, one of our professional service clients decided that it needed an organizational overhaul. Coordination of best practices and efficient and effective collaboration across service lines was dismal at best. Critical team members who needed to be at the edge of the business engaging current and prospective customers were anything but engaged. The client responded with a new organizational structure and drastically changed the work environment to support a community feel where service line subject matter experts were in close proximity to business development, marketing, and delivery resources. Team members could mingle and collaborate and engage customers easily, casually, and candidly in key discussion forums.

If you're trying to promote collaboration, as was the managing partner of this firm, proximity certainly helps, as does a visually appealing space. Unfortunately, in this case, it failed to spark any meaningful innovation or deeper relationships with key customers. Recently, management decided to revamp the organization and the workspace once again.

This example should ring with some familiarity to any organization that responds to sheer dysfunction without truly understanding its root causes. Decentralization, as mentioned earlier, could help organizational or leadership bottlenecks in decision making. But if you're struggling with poor or nonexisting communication, inflexibility, or lack of real collaboration from disparate sides of the organization, it's time to break down functional, geographic, or project-based silos.

Keep in mind that there is seldom a magic pill. The ideas by organizational effectiveness specialists look great on paper (believe me, I sat in a meeting with 12 of them recently at a Fortune 500 client), but they often produce disappointing results. Yet, like the blossom of the Japanese cherry trees on the Potomac River in Washington, D.C., each spring, reorganizations come and go with amazing regularity, often without significantly boosting the organization's effectiveness.

One of the inside jokes at Silicon Graphics (SGI) years ago was that, "It's not a reorg; it's a wardrobe," as evidenced by countless shirts from a multitude of three-letter divisional name changes that were so frequent, many in the field organization could seldom keep up. (We were all convinced that someone on the leadership team owned the promotional company that provided the plethora of trinkets.) Constant organizational changes seldom produce any real or lasting benefits for end customers.

Business Process Reengineering (BPR) and Total Quality Management (TQM) are two other common initiatives of the past that ignored the highly influential, yet nonorganizationally structured social networks of change agents. Knowledge sharing through collaboration is nearly impossible in isolation. In transforming an organization's willingness and ability to change, the relationships of those change agents are critical to anything actually getting accomplished.

Companies that invest resources such as time, talent, and capital to understand and leverage their intracompany, as well as externally influenced social networks, greatly improve their chances of creating lasting and highly impactful organizational and behavioral change through the leadership of their change agents. As a team, if the change agents can map critical, informal, yet highly influential networks and identify and leverage key connections—particularly across traditional organizational charts—they can independently isolate root causes; filter best in class options; mitigate risk through targeted pilot campaigns; and deliver small wins that can serve as momentum makers or future change shapers.

Beyond Influencers to the Influenced

As we discussed earlier, one of the best approaches to spreading a viral change campaign is to court key influencers. But recent research also confirms that the *influenced* may be as critical as the *influencers*. James Coyle, assistant professor of marketing at Miami University's Farmer School of Business, recently conducted a study that found that trying to track down key influencers—people who have extremely large social networks—can in some ways limit a campaign and its viral potential. Change agents instead need to realize that the majority of their audience, not just the well-connected few, is eager and willing to pass along well-designed and relevant messages.

Science News Online reports on related topical research by two social network theorists, Duncan J. Watts of Columbia University and Peter Sheridan Dodds of the University of Vermont in Burlington. These researchers tested the conventional wisdom that experts on a subject matter who love to talk can persuade dozens of others to adopt their opinions. If this were true, an excellent communication strategy would be to find those few critical people, convince them of the value of your change campaign, and leave it to them to persuade others.

Though this theory sounds good, it shouldn't be your only approach. The researchers compared how far an idea would spread depending on whether it started with a random individual or with an influential individual who was connected to a lot of other individuals. They found that highly influential individuals usually spread ideas more widely, but not *that* much more widely. More important than the influencers, the researchers found, were the *influenced*. Once an idea spread to a critical mass of easily influenced individuals, it quickly took hold and continued to spread to other easily influenced individuals.

Dodds compares the spread of ideas to the spread of a forest fire. When a fire turns into a conflagration, no one claims that it was because the spark that began it was so potent. Instead, a fire takes off because of the properties of the larger forest environment: dryness, density, wind, and temperature. So, what's the takeaway? According to the study, the best way to increase the odds of a person-to-person transmission of an idea is to make it a good idea. Some things are just fun to talk about. One of my favorite quotes by Seth Godin is to simply, "Be remarkable—that which is worthy of remark!"

Are your efforts to change an individual, a team, or the organization at large, worthy of remark? How can you ensure that beyond the network of influencers, the influenced are armed with just the right message to create the broad-based viral effect you need to broaden your reach and your return on impact?

Change through Mergers and Acquisitions

During a mergers and acquisitions event, both financial and strategic buyers rightly focus on the strategic, financial, and governance aspects of a transaction so as to further their goal of maximizing shareholder value. I recently met with a partner of a private equity firm who succinctly described the competency and capabilities of the group of professional services providers they use in both their pretransaction due diligence, as well as their postacquisition integration—what he referred to as his A-Team. From a global law firm to Big Four accounting, top-notch real estate agents, and a very recognizable retained search for the human capital component, they spare no expense in ensuring that world class teams are on their side of the table when pursuing strategic acquisitions.

Take one guess as to what's missing from this success formula? Someone to examine what ultimately becomes the greatest source of wealth creation—the strategic and quantifiable value of the relationships both inside, as well as outside the target acquisition companies. Is it any surprise then to learn that in the past year alone, three of this firm's portfolio companies have declared bankruptcy? Though there are certainly unique circumstances in each organization, when they announced the acquisition of each entity, it was the rage of the local business community. The lawyers and accountants had certainly done their part in the valuation of the hard assets. But the critical soft assets, such as discretely strained intracompany relationships between members of the leadership team; the dissatisfaction of their distribution channels with the direct sales model; and the lack of repeat or referral business from their vast customer base should have all been yellow flags to further investigate and certainly prioritize in their 100-Day Action Plans.

In our experience, conducting considerable due diligence regarding these relationships is as crucial as paying close attention to the balance sheet, cash flow, and expected synergies from the deal. By asking management a series of questions about their strategic relationships, investors can contribute to the smooth transition to a more unified company. This results in a better merging of the cultures, prevents the loss of A-Team players, and creates a stronger human capital bench for the joined entity—all of which will ultimately create far greater shareholder value from the transaction. Why, then, are these strategic relationships so often neglected?

During many roll-up opportunities, strategic and financial investors largely rely on bankers (often the chief advisers to the company) in the pending transaction. Understandably, investment bankers tend to focus on the financial aspects of the deal and believe that addressing the strategic relationship issue comes much later in the postacquisition integration process, if at all. As a result, the quantifiable and strategic value of these relationships is often grossly underestimated and their value can easily be disrupted if not destroyed in most common practices, after the merger and acquisition event.

Lack of Candor and Stand in Corporate America

A multitude of surveys done in the late 1960s showed that 70 percent of U.S. residents felt that corporations could generally be trusted to act responsibly. Even after the economic boom of the past two decades, this figure has fallen to around 45 percent.

Particularly, because of times of crisis for the business community and the demise of candor and trust, improvement in accepted practices and relationships among auditors, analysts, executives, and a multitude of stakeholders becomes difficult to visualize.

I believe many of us experience a very real lack of honesty in corporate America on a daily basis. I would submit that there is also very little *stand*. We're so conscious not to offend, not to polarize, not to leave anyone out, not to discriminate, and not to differentiate, that many of us go through a day, week, month, year, or lifetime without saying *anything* at all. If you don't stand for something, what *do* you believe in? What is it at your core that you are so fundamentally passionate about that you are willing to sacrifice a secure paycheck, benefits, and your precious vacation?

Relationship-Centric Best Practice: Protecting Unique Cultures

Kraft Foods Canada purchased a small West Coast coffee company with its own unique culture. The acquisition's ultimate success was largely due to executives at Kraft having graduated from the school of hard knocks in this area.

Kraft's sheer size and traditional approach to institutionalizing acquisitions could have proved detrimental, yet the upfront candor of the Kraft management team helped coffee company executives understand that Kraft was buying their brand, while at the same time adding its systems infrastructure and cultural best practices. By not painting a false picture of what was to remain true in the small company, Kraft avoided the possible misperceptions and consequently mass exodus of the critical human element of the coffee company.

In examining over 1,000 Match.com ads, brothers and authors of *Made to Stick,* Dan and Chip Heath, made an amazing discovery. Their research yielded clever headlines on personal ads such as, "*Hey*—If that's your opening line, you better be hot," and "Looking for Love—Duh! You're on Match.com." But even more striking was that well over 600 of the headlines simply said *nothing at all.*

For many, personal and functional interactions are very similar—they say nothing. Why? Mostly, it is because of *fear.* Fear of saying too much; fear of saying something clever that others may think is stupid; or fear of saying something relevant that some might find offensive. In an effort not to exclude anyone, we often succeed at boring everyone. The *hey* phenomenon is so prevalent in the corporate world that it is turning brands, which one could argue are a company's personal ad, into something very similar to the Match.com headlines that say nothing at all. In our world of "sound bites" in the context of building lasting relationships, there simply must be more.

Executives with the fiduciary responsibility to lead an organization have become so bland that you wonder who exactly, as a company, are they trying to date? In an effort to please everyone, they often succeed at engaging no one. Executives and their companies believe that with enough clout, scale, and arrogance, they can simply survive by being generically likeable. And for some, it may work—at least in the short term. But for the rest of us, almost everyone has to be ready to turn some people off.

If everyone refuses to discuss the elephant in the room, if mediocrity is not only tolerated, but accepted as the norm, and if the status quo is encouraged as not rocking the boat, isn't that just another version of, *hey?* The fear of being disliked afflicts many because of the greater perceived risk. Most executives fear that if they make a bold statement, they risk alienating customers, their bosses, and their boss's bosses. That fear ultimately takes the edge off the candor—the authenticity—and the core of that executive and the company.

Lack of Candor in Business Relationships

This same lack of candor resides in business relationships as well. Business leaders must commit to such transparency that a multitude of constituents will be empowered to make informed judgments beyond an acceptable level of scrutiny. Unfortunately, openly candid and honest dialog seems to elude many in our current business environment. Leaders have little incentive to make their operations more transparent because of an elongated, yet reasonable belief that they will be judged unfairly. Business relationships with the media point to great recent examples of companies fighting back when they believe their stories have been misrepresented or compromised.

I recall stories of Mobil Oil cutting all contact with the *Wall Street Journal* and withdrawing its advertising out of anger about news stories about the company. The Bechtel Group had ABC run a report disputing a *20/20* episode that wrongly accused the company. Illinois Power responded to a segment on CBS's *60 Minutes* by disseminating a videotape of their own that showed edited interviews with company executives. Yet, for some reason, this effort to fight back when you think you have been wronged doesn't manifest itself with intracompany or other externally focused business relationships.

Relationship-Centric Best Practice: Courage to Fail

Principal and founder of Talent Connections, LLC—a member of the coveted *Inc.* 500—and past president of SHRM Atlanta (Society of Human Resource Management) Tom Darrow shared with me a great reaffirming insight about candor and encouraging the courage to fail: As John Wayne once said, "Courage is being scared to death, but saddling up anyway." In many ways, candor also requires a built-in belief—not simply one of courage (how you

overcome barriers), but specifically, the courage to *fail*—
that which allows us to push the envelope to overcome critical limitations in our daily lives.

Tom referenced his efforts while playing tennis. When
he plays opponents of equal or lesser abilities, he said, his
game seldom improves. But when he is matched against
quicker, more agile players with crisper returns—particularly down the line—although he may never reach their
level, (and yes, even sometimes lose 6–1, 6–0), he plays a
much stronger game.

Getting people in an environment of candor must
begin with upper management. Their commitment to
openness and transparency goes a long way in helping the
rest of the organization to feel the same. With a plethora of
regulations from HIPAA to Sarbanes-Oxley, as well as competitive intelligence, upper management tends to believe
that intracompany information sharing should, in many
ways, remain on a need-to-know basis.

The fear of employee reactions, or worse yet, market
reaction to potentially bad news often keeps leadership
from sharing anything. And in the absence of information,
it is human nature to create imaginative stories in an effort
to fill the void.

Despite popular belief, most employees can hear and
see through a positive spin. More detrimental could be their
perception and a subsequent rippling effect that says,
in Tom's words, "Maybe I should start buttering up the
truth, too."

We meet seemingly nice people and despite a genuine initial interest, there just doesn't seem to be a viable mutual benefit
in investing in or nurturing the relationship. Yet, in an effort to
be nice and avoid hurting feelings, we are sheepish in our candor. We drag on unnecessary dialogs, personal exchanges, and

discussions of projects and opportunities with the exchange of pleasantries to avoid difficult conversations. For many, it is easier to simply ignore and procrastinate than it is to systematically address the elephant in the room.

When it comes to candor and accountability, I believe the number one accountability is still to yourself. There is a common misnomer that 21 days of repetition creates a habit. I'm not convinced it ever will. If you exercise for 253 consecutive days, and on day 254, you decide that you will not exercise that day, shouldn't the 21-day rule get you back in the saddle? Accountability and commitment is a core behavioral change versus one of finite time.

Not letting others down is a personal belief. By telling others that they can count on you and trust you, you must make the commitment to follow through. With accountability, focus, and commitment, you fulfill that obligation to self, which permeates in fulfilling your obligation to others. In essence, my candor and accountability to others sprouts from that committed seed of candor and accountability to myself.

Most would agree that—particularly as a leader—your actions speak far greater volume than your words. If subordinates continuously see or experience a conflict avoidance mentality in your business relationships, would you not agree that it will eventually dilute your credibility in their eyes?

100-Day Action Plan for Large-Scale Change or Mergers and Acquisitions

Why do you think most New Year resolutions don't stick? In one of my keynotes, someone suggested that it is because you are drunk when you make them. Beyond that theory, would you agree that they often include no accountability, realistic expectations, or systematic *plan*?

It has been said, "Teach and everyone will learn. Manage and no one will learn." One hundred days is simply too short a timeframe to correct any mistakes. As such, it is critical to start with three to five realistic goals with high impact potentials rather than try to hit an immediate home run.

In many ways, a 100-day plan is really a five-year plan compressed into 100 days. In any large-scale change or merger and acquisition event, orchestrating critical and timely information flow to the right people at the right time is critical and it would serve well to execute from a centralized program management office (PMO).

As described earlier, a succinct and quantifiable understanding of the impetus for change, whether a process, organization, or even change of control coupled with a strong change in the management team, is empowered by relationships of the change agents with the front line. A solid strategy will require a solidified plan for execution. Change fails not because someone miscalculated the math. In many cases, it is due to the underestimation of the human element and cultural attributes. Line executives who initiate change campaigns or put deals together, although astute in their business propositions, often miss the relationship ramifications.

In considering a 100-day action plan for large-scale change or merger and acquisitions events, there are three important phases:

Phase 1—Pretransaction Due Diligence

The organization must go into any proposed large-scale change or transaction with its eyes wide open and ask itself: What are we changing? What are we buying? Is this a good fit for the strategies of the business? Are we doing this for the right reasons? Are we running toward something or away from something else?

As mentioned earlier in this book, I believe that a *premortem* evaluation would save many teams and organizations unlimited levels of frustration and wasted resources. Peel back the organizational levels in search of fundamentally problematic areas such as redundant roles and responsibilities, compensation structures, or perhaps dormant litigation issues. Even in our small firm, our team spent an entire day at an offsite session contemplating whether a recent merger was congruent with our mission, vision, and beliefs—not just compatible with where our organization has been, but with where we are headed. Are their products and services consistent with our growth and sales strategies? Do we like their people and will our respective cultures thrive together under one roof? Are their synergies not only real, but also quantifiable? Will our coming together enhance a systematic approach for a greater return for our broad-based stakeholders?

Change will demand a deeper and broader leveraging of existing infrastructures. Identify where the weakest links are in those infrastructures and consider how you will retain them to protect the structural integrity of the organization.

It is also a very good idea to really think through how much this change or merger and acquisition is going to cost. Not just the obvious costs, but in potential areas such as relocation or enhancements of key assets (financial as well as human capital), severance for redundant resources, or closing of unnecessary facilities. And let us also not forget the opportunity costs and the focus that any kind of change will detract from one's normal course of business.

Phase 2—The First 100 Days

The first 100 days after a change or acquisition is announced significantly and unequivocally set the tone for what is to follow. It is critical that the organization leave the gate running. From that first minute, everyone wants to see action. Change isn't the decisions you've made up until this point; the organization wants to see them implemented.

The AlliedSignal-Honeywell merger is a good example of using the first 100 days to execute a great number of critical decisions. On Day One, the companies announced which facilities around the world would need to change or shut down. Specific, often painful decisions—many of which will require 50 to 60 subsequent decisions—must be made before that initial announcement. A half-baked plan will raise unnecessary alarms.

Specific programs to modify processes, relocate resources, and add or displace employees are all examples of decisiveness. When coupled with speed and communication, this will help people understand future direction. The faster you move, the more you'll build confidence for success in the organization.

It is critical to get not only senior leadership, but also one or two levels below, all on the same page. Get key issues on the table quickly and leverage a blueprint of a high performing organization to execute key processes and ensure traction with the execution of a multitude of simultaneous initiatives. If the senior team operates in a dysfunctional manner, it is not realistic to think that the cascading effect to the rest of the organization will somehow supersede it. This highly destabilizing time naturally makes people nervous. And relationships between peers, subordinates and superiors will help maintain morale, keep the focus on the actual business, and nurture the foundational trust on which it is critical to build.

Ignore the external facing parts of the organization and performance in the business will dramatically deteriorate. If the sales force either checks out or begins to leave, pending orders will be delayed and critical marketing and analyst relation campaigns for an upcoming major trade show may misstep, creating an unflattering or ambiguous buzz in the market.

We saw this firsthand in working with Scitex Vision, an Israeli-based global manufacturer of wide format digital printers. Some six to nine months in advance of the announced acquisition by HP, a number of critical clients with active deals on the table were reluctant to execute those much-needed purchase orders. This was primarily due to an uncertainty or doubt of the impending changes. Not knowing whether Kodak, Agfa, HP, Xerox, or countless others were going to acquire Scitex kept many suitors at bay and a sales force left scrambling to deliver on quota commitments.

People must focus on making decisions quickly and when a decision has not been made, senior leadership must demonstrate by telling people *when* it will be made. A simple approach to creating certainty in any relationship, and in particular during a time of highly disruptive transformation, is consistent communication as to when you can expect to know a prioritized set of real expectations. Leading by example includes reaching out to understand the new organization, producing concrete deliverables, and conservative/realistic timeframes for getting difficult work done. More so than ever, taking the time to meet, talk, and listen with key people will solidify respective expectations and build confidence and their buy-in as to the importance and direction of the pending changes.

The first 100 days also represents an incredible development opportunity, giving key people in one's Relationship Bank the positive experiences they will remember throughout their careers—not to mention publish on their resumes. For many, large change or merger and acquisition events are the Super Bowl, the World Series, the NBA Finals, and the Stanley Cup all merged into one. The right people on the bus will uncover new talents that they never knew they possessed. Only tough questions and real-time radar tracking the essential moving parts will ensure both sequential, as well as parallel, execution of significant milestones. Keep in mind that most people will prioritize requests for those they know, like, trust, and respect.

Phase 3—The Longer Term

After the initial 100 days, it is critical to devise a soul-searching litmus test for the entire organization. Beyond the initial shock and disbelief of the actual change, is the resulting organization their cup of tea? It's okay to come to the conclusion that the new people, processes, procedures, structure, attitude, or simply just the way things are done now isn't what they signed up for. It is not okay, however, to check out and forget to tell others.

Next, it is critical to review the organization's competency map after the dust has settled. Do we have the human capital needed to deliver long-term value? If the answer is anything but a resounding *Yes*, it is imperative to leverage critical intracompany relationships to extend your reach in the market and fill those gaps as diligently as you can.

In many cases, a post-100-day organization will continue to face a multitude of challenges. Only by being the positive force and continuing to bring people together will you uncover answers to unresolved questions. A Socratic leadership style of engaging the audience for their most pressing issues and openly, directly and transparently addressing those concerns will further solidify in people's minds that this really is a worthwhile home for their professional endeavors. Use town hall meetings, "Ask the CEO" campaigns, forums, intracompany blogs, and anonymous "call the CEO with an idea" as tools to embrace the far reaches of the business, remembering that it is incredibly difficult to be a remote employee.

10

The LinkedIn Effect

A re you LinkedIn? Do you Spoke, Ryze, Jigsaw, or ZoomInfo? Is this the year when you'll get a Second Life? If these social networking concepts are not on your radar, you are ignoring a dynamic trend that could have a profound impact on key areas of your business such as profitable revenue growth, talent acquisition, and operational efficiency and effectiveness. Web 2.0 landscape and practical applications of social networking technologies are enhancing individual, team-based, and organizationwide capabilities in the identification, development, and nurturing, as well as leveraging of strategic business relationships. (See Figure 10.1.)

At last count, over 300 social networking web sites exist in nine distinct categories:

- Business
- Common Interest

FIGURE 10.1 Social Networking Technology Tools.

- Dating
- Face-to-Face Facilitation
- Friends
- MoSoSo (Mobile Social Software)
- Pets
- Photos
- *Edge* Cases or Social Networking *Plus*

Our primary focus has remained upon the business applications of social networking technologies, although common interest applications are fueling real-time knowledge management (think of everyone in your organization struggling with complex project management initiatives or anyone who has ever researched a particular topic). Mobile applications are also becoming increasingly useful in large corporate campuses (think of SMS text alerts on your cell phone when someone you need to reach is in the same building).

A new evolution of Enterprise Relationship Management (ERM) applications has evolved encompassing research, connection engines, and relationship-matching capabilities to uncover previously unknown connections, primarily for business development purposes. These enabling technologies provide access to knowledge, talent, time, and most importantly, influential relationships.

Web 2.0

Consumer use and content-creation momentum on sites such as MySpace, YouTube, and Wikipedia are strong drivers of social networking technologies and online user collaboration initiatives such as blogs, forums, podcasts, and peer-to-peer networking sites—what is commonly referred to as *Web 2.0* in the business community. Our clients are beginning to view these technologies as a strategic asset in the development and nurturing of key relationships with customers and business partners. It is also a way to encourage collaboration and manage knowledge and just-in-time information flow with intracompany constituents as well. Achieving higher integration with suppliers and faster new product development and prototyping are also practical applications of Web 2.0 technologies.

Relationship-Centric Best Practice: Web 2.0 as Strategic Relationship Enablers

So what are some of the practical applications of Web 2.0 technologies? Here are nine applications that you can implement in your respective organizations, often from a grassroots level, because of their ease of implementation. These technologies are particularly successful when used as a pilot for a small group of users to gauge their long-term viability. As collaboration tools, they're also helping to break down traditional hierarchical barriers and functional or geographic boundaries when it comes to information flow.

1. *Blogs* (short for *web log*) are online journals or diaries hosted on a web site and often distributed to other sites or readers using RSS (see number 6). Some of the more interesting approaches are intracompany versions where anonymous users can post suggestions, ideas, and discussions forums—think of them as the much more capable suggestion boxes of the last two decades. Savvy clients interested in proactively nurturing their reputation capital are also using blogs to engage customers and critics with *positive* and *productive* discussions.

(continued)

Relationship-Centric Best Practice: Web 2.0 as Strategic Relationship Enablers (Continued)

2. *Collective Intelligence* refers to any system that attempts to tap the expertise of a group rather than an individual to make decisions. Technologies that contribute to collective intelligence include collaborative publishing and common databases for sharing knowledge. Mind maps are gaining particular popularity in brainstorming sessions.

3. *Mash-Ups* are aggregations of content from different online sources to create a new service. Clients are adding Google Maps to their online CRM tools for easy access to customer sites for field service calls.

4. *Peer-to-Peer Networking* (P2P) efficiently allows the sharing of files (music, videos, or text) broadly over the Internet or within a closed set of users. By distributing the files or even assembling them from a highly decentralized network, single points of failure and bottlenecks are eliminated. Savvy teams are also leveraging grid computing to utilize the untapped dormant systems in an organization (think about the collective and untapped computing power in the office at nights or on weekends).

5. *Podcasts*, popularized by Apple and iTunes, also have a strong corporate function as a multimedia provider of distributed content to a broad audience. Years ago, SGI Silicon Studio would distribute audio cassettes to the field sales organization that described the previous month's best practices. The same function could be much more easily produced and distributed today through podcasts.

6. *RSS* (Really Simple Syndication) allows individuals to subscribe to online aggregators and distributors of news, blogs, podcasts, or other information highly

customized for their topics of interest. Imagine getting only the sections of the *Wall Street Journal* that you care about. Or better yet, instead of reams of monthly reports, how about an RSS of just the manufacturing or marketing updates from each functional executive?

7. *Social Networking* refers to platforms that allow users to build a professional profile and share common interests, knowledge, talent, or simply preferences. LinkedIn, ZoomInfo, Spoke, and Facebook Corporate are some examples of what our clients are using within their organizations for business development, recruiting, and due diligence purposes.

8. *Web Services* are intelligent wirings of disparate applications, allowing them to exchange information and conduct transactions. These services have replaced many of the traditional EDI (electronic data interface) functionalities of the past two decades. Clients in the retail industry are able to use Web services to update their inventory systems or delivery schedules.

9. *Wikis,* such as Wikipedia, are environments for collaborative publishing. They allow many authors to contribute to an online document or discussion stream, although the authenticity or credibility of the content is questionable at times. These applications are gaining strong momentum within organizations for highly decentralized knowledge management applications. Wikis are particularly useful in capturing highly unstructured or anecdotal information.

Web-based customer relations management systems allow a multitude of constituents to quickly learn customer preferences and leverage recommendations from various support functions on opportunities to improve the overall customer experience.

With Web 2.0 applications, the information flow no longer needs to travel through a series of filtered layers within the organization to reach those at the front line whom it can help the most. Organizations that create a legal and ethical framework, but otherwise allow the candid and open (anonymity helps) dialog on Web 2.0 platforms within the organization, are optimistic about their contributions to refining the business strategy and closing the gap with execution.

Organizations that create an open forum for dialog with business partners and customers are getting much more real-time input on a multitude of topics such as product design suggestions and customer service best practices such as *click-to-call* or *click-to-chat* applications. If you get something wrong, the customers will let you know very quickly, which allows the much needed agility to make quick decisions and improve profitable growth.

Reverse Mentoring to Gain Critical Mass

Although grassroots efforts are an effective get-out-of-the-gate strategy, once the real collaborative value of these applications are proven, they often garnish the support of the much needed internal champions who continue to invest in their design, development, and deployment. In many client cases, top-down management would have delayed pilot projects or created bureaucratic hindrance. One *Fortune* 500 client was savvy enough to understand that the senior leaders were not of the right mindset to embrace these next-generation applications, so we worked with them to develop a reverse-mentoring program. Each quarter, we polish the most promising 20-something to go to the top floor and demonstrate the practical applications of Web 2.0 technologies to senior leaders and board members. The senior management's role then becomes one of providing permission, boundaries, and resources for successful deployment of such innovation by intelligent and vested teams. "Son, I didn't understand half of what you just showed us, but if it'll help run this business better, I recommend we go ahead. Just behave yourself," is a paraphrased quote I've heard after a demonstration of a highly decentralized wiki to a group of board members.

Overcoming Traditional Barriers to Adoptions

The ability to quickly marshal resources and develop functional prototypes eliminates much of the traditional technology adoption barriers. Usability testimonials from actual users—for example, one customer e-mailed a VP of customer service about how much easier she found the avatar (intelligent, 3D digital character) in resolving her particular situation—support this notion. Passion and inspiration—and perhaps a bit of aspiration as well—by key natural users continue to drive the introduction of Web 2.0 technologies in a multitude of client environments.

An interesting perspective is that many of these innovative stakeholders come from other companies or perhaps even other industries—a beverage branding expert goes to a hotel company and spearheads the use of Second Life as a tool to prototype new room layouts and styles for online business customer testing. The *cool factor* in drag and drop graphics and highly engaging audio and video provide a very different definition, delivery, and acceptance of information. This is often the very impetus the organization needs to take the leap. Even the highly conservative SunTrust Bank recently demonstrated a Second Life island for training and development simulation at a senior leadership gathering. You can't access it from work, but when you go home, you can get online and check out the cool scenery.

Some industries are ripe for embracing social networking technologies. Numerous highly customized social networking technology platforms are helping clients in the media (newspapers and magazines in particular), sports (major leagues, individual teams, and online fantasy teams), as well as associations where there is a need to not only continue to attract a new generation of customers, but those with extensive commonalities. Unfortunately, some shareholders continue to see these applications as a cost versus an opportunity. While the transformation of the business to a more relationship-centric model is critical, without an engaged public who is willing and able to pay for the necessary infrastructure investments (in forms of ads and more prevalent purchases of products or services from online content providers), adoption, although necessary, will continue to be sluggish.

Return on Impact from Social Networking Technologies

It is simply too soon to measure the quantifiable impact of many Web 2.0 technologies in the market today. Client executives are documenting, however, improved customer service response rates, frequency, and quality of information and knowledge flow between internal teams, and a more proactive management of the company's reputation by the product marketing and brand management teams. One interesting aspect has become known as Sales 2.0. An average B2B sales professional can schedule between 7 and 10 face-to-face meetings per week using traditional prospecting approaches. But by using applications such as LinkedIn and Jigsaw to penetrate an account and online collaboration tools such as WebEx or GoToWebinar, sales efforts can increase to 30-plus prospect visits per week, although many are virtual. This clearly demonstrates the increasing immediate value while mitigating risk. According to CSO Insights, in many industries where sales efficiency and effectiveness is heavily driven by optimized mathematical formulas, a 5 percent increase in any of the key variables such as prospecting or proposing can produce significantly higher returns of closed business.

While many executives choose to invest in renewed processes and emerging technologies as a competitive advantage or to reduce operating costs, Web 2.0 applications have been found to be most valuable for collaborative purposes both inside as well as outside the organization. This is often seen by the strengthening of Relationship Currency investments, the nurturing of respective Relationship Banks, and the overall cultivation of critical relationships between suppliers, distribution channel partners, and end customers. A stronger, more engaged, and collaborative community, powered by Web 2.0 applications, requires less marketing campaign push and benefits from an accelerated customer perspective that the organization is reducing its self-interest in the interest of providing subject matter or domain expertise to its high value constituents.

LinkedIn as the Dominant Social Networking Platform for Professionals

The dynamic favor economy is the core motivator of the 22 million and exponentially growing user base in more than 170 industries that has converged on LinkedIn—a single online platform for professionals that didn't exist until just a few years ago. Although many leaders have heard of LinkedIn, there are still a good amount who are either under the impression that it's a fad that will fade away or that it has little bearing on them personally or professionally. What they neglect to realize is that 499 of the *Fortune* 500 companies currently have director-level profiles and higher on LinkedIn. Even Barack Obama recently teamed up with LinkedIn to reach entrepreneurs and small business owners and executives, asking them very pointed questions regarding their needs from the next U.S. president.

LinkedIn is a place to find and leverage professional opportunities, both now and throughout the course of one's career. LinkedIn enables individuals to:

- Present themselves and their professional capabilities
- Find and reconnect with past colleagues and classmates

- Leverage powerful tools to find and reach the people they need
- Build a powerful network of trusted professionals
- Discover professional relationships and opportunities
- Tap in to inside connections and uncover information

Whether you seek a job, a hire, a reference, a sales lead, an expert, or an inside connection at one of 70,000 companies, LinkedIn is an irreplaceable resource for building your professional relationships and achieving your goals.

Similarly to how referrals and trusted introductions are made in the real world, social networking web sites such as LinkedIn allow you to automate and exponentially enhance your current relationship reach. More important, these sites enhance and accelerate the quantifiable *value* of that expansion. They allow you to expand your portfolio of relationships *and* get more out of it. In my experience, there are generally four types of LinkedIn users:

1. Those who have *no idea* what LinkedIn is!
2. *Beginners* who continue to receive invites to "Join My Network" and keep deleting them!
3. *Intermediate* users who have a profile and maybe even a few connections, and visit the site periodically, but have yet to find a way to really get the most out of this amazing technology.
4. *Advanced* users who are savvy about their profiles, make appropriate connections and recommendations, are typically premium users, and are leveraging their business relationships toward execution, performance, and results.

Although many use this tool to build their networks, a much stronger asset is to *enhance* that network and derive Relationship Economics from the diversity and quality of those trusted relationships.

Using LinkedIn to Accelerate the Relationship Currency Road Map

If you have attended any of my keynote speeches or Relationship Economics training courses, you have heard our fundamental belief in the Relationship Currency Road Map. (See Figure 10.2.) It simply states that:

- If you start by making impactful deposits . . .
- for a key member of your Relationship Bank,
- it will earn you access to or an opportunity with a Pivotal Contact,
- Which will accelerate your ability to achieve your Relationship-Centric Goals.

  Said another way:
- What are you trying to accomplish?
- Who do you need?

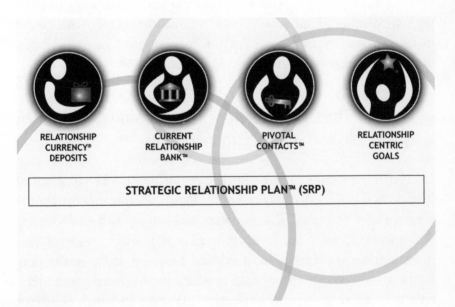

FIGURE 10.2 Relationship Currency Road Map.

- Who do you know?
- How can you add value to those you already know to create access to those you need to achieve your goals and objectives?

The basic tenet of business relationships is one of value-added interactions and reciprocity in the perceived value delivered. If you recall, the definition of *Relationship Currency deposits* is simply:

- Knowledge or talent (see LinkedIn *Answers* tab, where you can respond intelligently to questions asked)
- Time (Outlook toolbar/dashboard)
- Introduction to influential relationships (developing, nurturing, and extreme protection of your most trusted relationships)

If you begin by defining and solidifying the process, LinkedIn becomes an incredibly valuable tool to automate a great process. Conversely, if you start inviting and attempting to connect with others haphazardly, you will unfortunately—like most novice LinkedIn users—see little to no benefit from your business-to-business social networking efforts.

The LinkedIn Effect in Professional Service Organizations

LinkedIn continues to provide very real value to a broad array of professional service organizations. From accounting to PR to creative and IT consulting, professional service firms of varying size and geography are leveraging this platform to address two pressing needs: strengthening existing business and winning new business. We've identified and coached professional service clients in the five simple, yet effective manners in which they can strengthen their functional and strategic business relationships.

Get Visible—Similarly to Google, prospective clients find your content-rich LinkedIn profile when it matches a keyword search term they use. It is critical to update your professional bio and include past successful client engagements, industry associations, as well as civic and community involvements. With millions of searches performed monthly on LinkedIn, there is a good chance your expertise has already been searched a few times. Are you showing up in the results for prospective clients to contact you?

Search and Research—LinkedIn allows you to find managers in a particular industry or region, which enables you to identify new prospects, particularly among former colleagues and clients. If you nurtured those relationships in the past, LinkedIn is a great mechanism to get reengaged and caught up on both sides. When conducting due diligence on existing or prospective clients, most web sites share where the organization *has been*, but seldom provide you with any insights on where they're *headed*. Only by independently identifying and engaging key client contacts and influencers in your target organizations, will you be able to extract valuable insights regarding future opportunities to affect their business. LinkedIn helps you find these key pivotal contacts and reach them through introductions made by your existing Relationship Bank.

Get introduced—Many professional service providers get the majority of their clients through word-of-mouth referrals. By connecting on LinkedIn with trusted professionals with whom you've worked in the past, or those who have referred opportunities to you previously, you create the avenues to make Relationship Currency deposits, while arming them with your information and asking for a kind introduction to the key individuals you want to reach.

Get Endorsed—A solid approach to establishing your Reputation Capital within LinkedIn is to get endorsements from former clients and colleagues whom you've impressed with the quality and diversity of your performance and work ethics.

Given the competitive professional service arena, testimonial snippets reaffirm your competency and capabilities and can be added to your profile for a strong presentation and validation of relevant applications of your expertise. Aim to diversify the sources and types of project success stories and to reciprocate recommendations of past and present colleagues and fellow professional service providers whose work you've appreciated in the past.

Get Answers—LinkedIn Answers provides a platform for a highly decentralized knowledge management process. An effective strategy to solidify your subject matter expertise is to offer solutions and answers or to recommend an expert to specific questions posted by your Relationship Bank online. Beyond adding value to each interaction, this approach also strengthens your Reputation Capital by establishing you as the go-to resource on particular topics or situations. We've also been able to turn answers into alliance relationships as well thought out and highly credible responses point to a previously untapped source of expertise for longer-term relationships versus the instant gratification of a question answered.

Relationship-Centric Best Practice: LinkedIn Answers

As part of a global survey, Shel Israel, author of *Naked Conversations,* posted the following question on LinkedIn Answers as well as his blogosphere: *How do you think social media will impact business in the next five years?* Below is a sampling of the answers to his question.

"Internally, firms can and are better leveraging their internal resources by providing them the tools and contexts to collaborate more powerfully. This is a particular challenge in larger firms where they may have tremendous knowledge resources that are not being leveraged to the fullest. Externally, some firms (in both B-to-B and B-to-C environments) are leveraging social networks as an innovative process that helps them bring better products and services to a market interested in buying them."

— *Gregg Gallagher, Director of Marketing Practice at Quantum Leaders*

"I think the impact will be huge. I think there is a huge shift in how people seek, access, and interact with information and communities. I think business and government are going to need to change their approaches and interactions.

I also think they know how business promotes their products and services, and their companies will continue to change as the Web moves from a traditional passive experience to one that is more active and relationship-based."

— *Kevin Novak, Director of Web Services at the Library of Congress*

"Businesses will take social media increasingly seriously over the next five years, but where they insert it into their communications strategies is the question. Does it fall under the purview of the marketers? That is, is it more properly a 'direct marketing' exercise, because an increasing amount of this media will be consumer-generated? Or, because it is 'media,' is it still to be tasked to the corporate communications and public relations specialists to be sorted out? And, will this be the case as social media consolidation and merging with other, more traditional platforms continues?"

— *Michael Tangeman, VP, Pen Group Communications*   (*continued*)

Relationship-Centric Best Practice:
LinkedIn Answers (Continued)

"Companies are made up of people who are learning to adapt to a world where everybody is connected, everybody contributes, and everybody is zero distance (or close enough) from everybody else. This is the 'flat world' Tom Friedman wrote about, and he's right."

—Doc Searls, Senior editor, Linux Journal and owner of the Searls Group

"Radical transparency will lead to meritocracy, improved products and improved customer service, increased focus by companies on brand management, and a greater adoption of open standards by companies leading to greater buy-in from consumers."

—Tom Raftery, Founder of Tom Raftery IT

The LinkedIn Effect in the Venture Capital Community

In our experience, the following key factors heavily influence the results of many venture capital investments:

- Selection and on-boarding of high quality, high-performance-minded entrepreneurs
- Quality, speed, and convenience of high value interactions
- Attracting and retaining the right professional managers at the right time in the emerging growth company's life cycle
- Appropriate and highly relevant deal-filtering mechanism
- Highly diverse and thorough due diligence process
- Improved quality and quantity of deal flow
- Adding valuable board members to portfolio companies

If you agree, then LinkedIn may be a solid approach to each of these attributes. Here's how.

Selection and on-boarding of high quality, high-performance-minded entrepreneurs—Get references on prospective entrepreneurs from your Relationship Bank. Traditional inquiries as to who used to work with a prospective entrepreneur is time and resource intensive. A targeted search on the company, geography, and key roles makes this search simple. A profile on LinkedIn, as well as insights from past colleagues, can also help you more effectively plan for their selection, assessment, and on-boarding process.

Quality, speed, and convenience of high value interactions—Reverse or backdoor references are just a few clicks away with LinkedIn. And because access to these pivotal contacts is granted through your Relationship Bank, they're not only more likely to be candid, but will refer you to a broader set of potential references. Former managers, colleagues, investors, customers, suppliers, and strategic alliances can all provide quality conversations at a fraction of traditional outreach campaigns.

Attracting and retaining the right professional managers at the right time—Every emerging growth company goes through a natural life cycle that requires very different skill sets of its leaders. Few leaders possess the same focus, tenacity, and the relationships to succeed from zero to $1 million or $5 million in revenue as they do from $500 million to $2 billion-plus. Getting the right executive at the right time can often make or break a company. Recruiters may or may not be able to provide the right fit. Connecting on LinkedIn with highly trusted portfolio or 2 A.M. contacts in your Relationship Bank (see Chapter 7: Relationship Value Pyramid)—people who know you and your requirements for a particular company's hands-on leadership needs, may be very effective in identifying someone with the whole package to lead your portfolio companies.

Appropriate and highly relevant deal filtering mechanism—Many VC firms focus their investment opportunities through highly filtered selection criteria. It often compromises sweet spots in investment dollars over the lifetime of the investment, and includes particular industries, geographies, or solutions complementary to their existing portfolio companies for expanded economies of scope and scale. Many of the same criteria could be researched on LinkedIn for experts in various fields, cross-references of entrepreneurs' skills and accomplishments (or the entire management team's for that matter), and insights on key industry trend challenges or opportunities.

Highly diverse and thorough due diligence process—By leveraging the keyword functionality in LinkedIn, you can identify knowledgeable experts in areas such as *Active RFID*, *WiMax*, *VoIP*, or *Metadata*. You can review their profiles online to identify the most relevant experts and reference them through key members of your Relationship Bank. You can research customers using the solutions of your target portfolio investment and validate market traction (it is amazing how often *paying customers* is the only market validation that really matters). Did they have the problems your passionate entrepreneur articulated and is there really a sense of urgency to invest in a solution to resolve it? The solution may otherwise prove to be an expensive science project.

Improved quality and quantity of deal flow—Searching competitive or possible alliance partnerships for your current or prospective portfolio companies has often proved invaluable in uncovering hidden niche opportunities. One VC client stumbled on a conversation with an expert at a company where he was working on a unique solution. Through an introduction to an angel investor, a new entity was formed and serial entrepreneurs added to the mix to transform the original founder's technical idea into a product, and a product into a new company. The VC stayed in touch throughout the process and recently led an $8 million, A-round investment into the 18-month-old company.

Adding great board members to your portfolio companies—In our experience, highly experienced and relevant board members with market, domain, or industry experience can help serve as an independent sounding board and governance resource for fledging entrepreneurs and their growing companies. If you begin by clearly understanding the board talent the portfolio company needs today, as well as appreciating how those requirements will change over the next 18 to 36 months, LinkedIn becomes a great resource for identifying seasoned board members and getting their unique perspectives and insights on the portfolio company.

We recommend that VC and entrepreneur clients alike conduct the same level of due diligence on board members as on any other human capital asset and outline their compensation based on the operating plan requirements and performance targets of the portfolio company.

Relationship-Centric Best Practice: Community of Portfolio Companies

Venture capital or private equity portfolio companies, although potentially very diverse in their solution offerings and go-to-market strategies, often share an extremely similar set of profitable revenue growth, talent acquisition and development, and operational efficiency and effectiveness challenges. As such, we've worked with a number of VCs and PEGs in creating both a community of portfolio company relationships and content for their annual gatherings of senior leaders. Here are some examples of how to leverage LinkedIn to enhance that community and leverage shared best practices both inside and outside individual portfolio companies.

- *Connect Portfolio Company CEOs*—Give them a chance to connect online, review respective profiles, and uncover opportunities to become an asset to one another.

(continued)

**Relationship-Centric Best Practice:
Community of Portfolio Companies (Continued)**

- *Connect to Sources of Quality Deal Flow*—They'll be protective of their Reputation Capital with you and are likely to forward relevant deals for your review.

- *Connect and Recommend Trusted Service Providers*—Tom Beaty of Insight Sources, Bishop Leatherbury of Tatum Partners, and David Rubenstein of the Miller-Richmond Company have been able to create great value for a multitude of portfolio companies; connecting them to other portfolio company executives and expediting access to trusted sources through critical phases of the portfolio company's growth.

- *Encourage Proactive Participation*—Social networking technologies such as LinkedIn deliver exponential value through viral use. The more active members from various portfolio companies who join, the higher the likelihood of creating valuable connections, forwarding critical requests, and facilitating value-added relationship interactions.

- *Set up a Private LinkedIn Group*—Think of this as a subgroup of the portfolio company's management teams, trusted service providers, executives, and knowledge resources. They can contact one another without requiring a LinkedIn introduction and begin to share critical best practices across the entire portfolio.

Technology as a Dual-Edged Sword

Over the years, I've been blessed with a great lifestyle from and around the technology field. From ComputerLand in the 1980s to Silicon Graphics in the 1990s and SaaS (Software as a Service) applications since 2000, I've seen the amazing evolution of a multitude of information technology advances. They were all introduced with the intentions of helping us share not just data, but insights, and as a way to collaborate around global best practices and optimize the manner in which we get things done. Although I'm passionate about technology (as evidenced by the purchase of my sixth Blackberry device in the past 12 years), I fear that technology is in many ways contributing to our societal disconnect. Walk into any Starbucks location and it's filled with people, all heads down working on their laptops or mobile devices, in an environment ideally suited for engaging others. If we can have very productive virtual meetings on Second Life, why can't we take the time to engage one another in person?

If text messaging is defining your relationships with others, how will you ever *really* get to know and engage them beyond the cryptic, twenty-first-century version of hieroglyphics? LOL, 4COL, D00d, A3, LQTM, MYOB, RME, PROLLY, G/F, KEWL, QT, K. If you're really confused, here is the dictionary for the rest of us:

- LOL—Laugh Out Loud
- 4COL—For Crying Out Loud
- D00d—Dude
- A3—Anytime, Anywhere, Anyplace
- LQTM—Laughing Quietly to Myself
- MYOB—Mind Your Own Business
- RME—Rolling My Eyes
- PROLLY—Probably
- G/F—Girlfriend
- KEWL—Cool
- QT—Cutie
- K—Okay

Technology is an enabler to relationship development—it is never its replacement. Nothing will ever replace a personal touch, a warm smile, or a comforting soul. E-learning has never really taken off to expected levels because nothing will ever substitute for the knowledge, expertise, and most importantly, the ability to touch, influence, motivate, inspire, and engage the audience than that person at the front of the room. As an admitted Blackberry addict (many call it a *Crackberry*), I'm working hard not to jump every time it buzzes. I have committed to simply turning it off during family times and leaving it behind on weekends and vacations. Technology should help us do the heavy lifting in identifying, building, and nurturing our most valuable relationships. It should never replace it.

Final Thoughts

I know you had a lot of reading choices and whether you purchased this book or if it was given to you, I'm grateful for the gift of your time. I hope you found the content of interest and value—whether as a reminder of the critical importance of relationships you already possess or some new insights on how to more intentionally, strategically, and thus quantifiably transform your most valuable business contacts into personal and professional success. Keep in mind several of the key concepts.

- There is a Grand Canyon–sized difference between knowing relationships are important and doing the right things and doing them now.
- You may know that relationships are critical, but is it cascading down to your respective teams?
- As a society, we're becoming increasingly disconnected and in many ways, we're losing our ability to engage people—those who will make decisions to work with us, support us, help us, work for us, and go above and beyond the call of duty on our behalf. They do this not simply

because of our authority, but because they know, like, trust, and respect us.

- People can't trust you unless you give them an opportunity to get to know you. Give them the chance to do just that and get to know who they are, not simply what they do.
- Relationships are an investment. Read the prospectus, aim to enhance your portfolio of relationships, and diversify and build for quality, not just quantity. Throw away the stopwatch and get a compass!
- Influence the conversations and you'll influence the relationships. Influence the relationships and you'll influence the outcomes you desire.
- You don't have the bandwidth to invest in everyone equally, so how will you prioritize your most valuable relationships?
- It's never about the coffee or the meal. It's about an opportunity to engage others and not only strengthen your existing Relationship Bank, but expand your portfolio of pivotal contacts.
- You can't possibly improve anything you don't measure. Value pyramid your current relationships and identify those critical and most instrumental to your success—both today as well as in the future.
- Your 2 A.M.s and Joans will help you think big and constantly raise the bar on your personal and professional development.

Here's to your strategic relationship success!
David
www.relationshipeconomics.NET/nour.html

About the Author

About the founder of Relationship Economics:

David Nour, CEO—BeOne Now, Inc.
David Nour is a social networking strategist and one of the foremost thought leaders on the quantifiable value of business relationships. In a global economy that is becoming increasingly disconnected, BeOne Now, Inc. is solving *Fortune* 500 client challenges with intracompany, as well as externally focused, Strategic Relationship Planning—the process of transforming valuable business relationships into execution, performance, and results.

A native of Iran, David came to the United States with a suitcase, $100, limited family ties and no fluency in English! Over the past two decades, he has built an impressive career of entrepreneurial success, both within large corporations and early-stage ventures.

David is a senior management adviser and featured keynote speaker for corporate, association, and academic forums, where he shares his knowledge and experience as a leading change agent and visionary for Relationship Economics—the art and science of relationships.

In addition to serving his community as a former board member of the Center for Puppetry Arts and a former co-chair of the United Way Tech Initiative, The Bridge, and High Tech Ministries, David is also an active member of several professional organizations, including the Association for Corporate Growth (ACG), American Management Association (AMA), Institute of

Management Consultants (IMC), and the Society of International Business Fellows (SIBF).

In the past, David was named to *Georgia Trend*'s 40 Under 40, *Atlanta Business Chronicle*'s Up and Coming, and Who's Who in Atlanta Technology awards. He has been featured in a variety of publications, including the *Wall Street Journal*, the *New York Times*, the *Atlanta Journal and Constitution*, the *Atlanta Business Chronicle*, *SmartMoney.com*, *Forbes Small Business*, *Georgia Trend*, *Entrepreneur*, and *Pink* magazines.

David earned an Executive MBA from the Goizueta Business School at Emory University where he's often a guest lecturer, and a BA degree in management from Georgia State University. He currently resides with his family in Atlanta, Georgia.

Index